# CLASSICAL COMICS STUDY GUIDE

Making Shakespeare accessible
for teachers and students

Suitable for KS2 and KS3

Written by: Jason Cobley

## THE GRAPHIC NOVEL
William Shakespeare

# CLASSICAL COMICS STUDY GUIDE

Henry V: The Graphic Novel

First UK Edition

Published by: Classical Comics Ltd

Written by: Jason Cobley

Pencils: Neill Cameron    Inks: Bambos
Colouring: Jason Cardy & Kat Nicholson

Acknowledgments: Every effort has been made to trace
copyright holders of material reproduced in this book. Any rights
not acknowledged here will be acknowledged in subsequent
editions if notice is given to Classical Comics Ltd.

All enquiries should be addressed to:
Classical Comics Ltd.
PO Box 7280
Litchborough
Towcester
NN12 9AR, UK
Tel: 0845 812 3000

education@classicalcomics.com
**www.classicalcomics.com**

ISBN: 978-1-906332-07-5

Printed in the UK

# CONTENTS

# INTRODUCTION

## WELCOME TO THE HENRY V STUDY GUIDE FROM CLASSICAL COMICS.

This photocopiable resource is designed with ease of use in mind. We have all seen study guides that provide a great deal of information but provide little in terms of enjoyable activities for children to engage with. Yet another one of those wouldn't be of any use to a busy teacher, so what we hope we have managed to achieve here is a focus on fun as well as learning.

This resource can be used alongside the Classical Comics adaptation as well as any traditional text, although that definitely isn't a requirement. In fact, many of the activities can stand on their own as introductions to the world of Shakespeare. It can also be used in conjunction with the Classical Comics whiteboard resource.

Most of the activities look at Shakespeare's use of language, but you will also see applications for history, ICT, drama, and art.

**"Thus far with rough, and all-unable pen,
Our bending author hath pursu'd the story..."**

Jason Cobley

Jason Cobley has taught English in a variety of secondary schools and sixth forms for a number of years, eight of them as Head of English. He currently leads a department at a school in Cambridgeshire. Jason is also a Senior Examiner for AQA GCSE English. As a writer, Jason self-published the comic strip adventures of Captain Winston Bulldog for many years and most recently, Jason has written the graphic novel adaptation of Mary Shelley's "Frankenstein" for Classical Comics, and this study guide.

Website: www.jasoncobley.blogspot.com
Contact: jasoncobley@gmail.com

# SHAKESPEARE TIMELINE

| Approx. Dates | Plays | What happened at the time? |
|---|---|---|
| 1564 | | William Shakespeare was born in Stratford-Upon-Avon on 23rd April. |
| 1572 | | Shakespeare possibly started at the New King's School grammar school in Stratford. |
| 1582 | | Shakespeare married Ann Hathaway. By 1585 they had 3 children. |
| 1586 - 1592 | Maybe Shakespeare started writing his poetry here. No one knows when he did them. By 1601 he had written these poems:<br>VENUS AND ADONIS<br>THE RAPE OF LUCRECE<br>SONNETS<br>A LOVER'S COMPLAINT<br>THE PHOENIX AND THE TURTLE | Nobody knows! Some people think that he travelled abroad, or that he was a teacher, or that he ran away from Stratford because he was in trouble for stealing a deer! He may have been one of The Queen's Men group of actors. In 1592 to the playwright Robert Greene called Shakespeare an "upstart crow". He was jealous of the brilliant new writer! |
| 1593 | | Shakespeare's friend and fellow playwright Christopher Marlowe is killed in a tavern in Deptford. All the theatres were shut because of the plague. |
| Before 1594 | HENRY VI (three parts)<br>RICHARD III<br>TITUS ANDRONICUS<br>LOVE'S LABOURS LOST<br>THE TWO GENTLEMEN OF VERONA<br>THE COMEDY OF ERRORS<br>THE TAMING OF THE SHREW | Shakespeare joined The Lord Chamberlain's Men company of actors when the theatres reopened. |
| 1594 - 1597 | ROMEO AND JULIET<br>A MIDSUMMER NIGHT'S DREAM<br>RICHARD II<br>KING JOHN<br>THE MERCHANT OF VENICE | About this time, we think that Shakespeare wrote LOVE'S LABOURS WON, but the play has been lost! |
| 1597 - 1600 | HENRY IV part i<br>HENRY IV part ii<br>HENRY V<br>MUCH ADO ABOUT NOTHING<br>MERRY WIVES OF WINDSOR<br>AS YOU LIKE IT<br>JULIUS CAESAR<br>TROILUS AND CRESSIDA | In 1597, Shakespeare bought a house in Stratford. In 1598, The Theatre in London burned down. In 1599, just after he finished Henry V, Shakespeare's company had The Theatre rebuilt as The Globe. |
| 1601 - 1608 | HAMLET<br>TWELFTH NIGHT<br>MEASURE FOR MEASURE<br>ALL'S WELL THAT ENDS WELL<br>OTHELLO<br>KING LEAR<br>MACBETH<br>TIMON OF ATHENS<br>ANTONY AND CLEOPATRA<br>CORIOLANUS | Queen Elizabeth I died in 1603. James VI became James I of England and Wales. King James became the patron of Shakespeare's company The King's Men, which means he had Royal support. In 1605, Guy Fawkes tried to blow up Parliament. |
| After 1608 | PERICLES<br>CYMBELINE<br>THE WINTER'S TALE<br>THE TEMPEST<br>HENRY VIII | In 1613, The Globe burned down, then was rebuilt in 1614. Shakespeare retired to Stratford and did some writing with John Fletcher, his successor in The King's Men. He died in 1616. In 1623, his plays were published in the First Folio. |

# THE GLOBE THEATRE

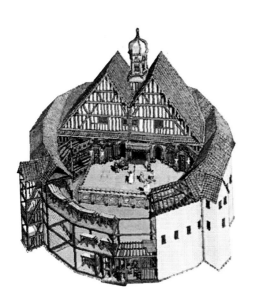

The first proper theatre in England was called The Theatre. Owned by James Burbage, it was built at Shoreditch, London in 1576. Before this playhouse was built, plays were performed outside inns or sometimes in the houses of rich people. Imagine seeing a play in a pub car park or in your sitting room! The Theatre was a big success and the Rose Theatre (1587) and the Hope Theatre (1613) followed. When The Theatre burned down in 1599, The Globe Theatre was built by Shakespeare's acting company in Southwark, London.

The Globe was the most magnificent theatre ever seen in London. It could hold thousands of people and didn't just show plays. It is rumoured that it was also a gambling house!

Plays were very popular and there was money to be made. Theatres would compete with each other and there was a constant demand for new material. As soon as a play was written, it was printed and put on stage straight away. Theatres would steal each other's ideas all the time. In fact, theatres were so popular that a law was introduced in 1591 to close them on a Thursday so that bull and bear bating could still go on! Shakespeare could barely keep up, so sometimes the actors only had parts of the script to work from, called 'foul papers'. They often didn't even know what parts they were playing until the day of the performance and they would have to perform ten different plays in a week. There were no female actors. Only men were allowed to act, so all female parts had to be played by men. Two of the most famous actors at the time were Edward Alleyn and Will Kempe, who became very rich by investing in the theatre company The Admiral's Men.

When a play was about to start, the grounds surrounding the Globe Theatre would have been bustling with people. There would be market stalls outside and people would avoid work to go. The atmosphere would be like a football match today! The Latin motto of the Globe was "Totus mundus agit histrionem" (the whole world is a playhouse). Shakespeare used this in As You Like It , when he wrote the phrase "All the world's a stage".

The common people (called groundlings) would pay one penny to stand in the 'pit' of the Globe. They had to put the money in a box as they went in. This is where we get the term 'box office' from! The rich people would pay to sit comfortably in the galleries. Theatre performances were held in the afternoon, because no one had discovered electricity or gas yet to be able to light it inside at night. In 1593, 1603 and 1608 all theatres were closed due to the Bubonic Plague (The Black Death). This was probably when Shakespeare did most of his writing.

# THE NEW GLOBE

Although the original Globe Theatre no longer exists, it is possible to now go to see a play in the same way that the Groundlings did in Shakespeare's day!

Shakespeare's Globe is a famous theatre that exists today in London at Bankside on the River Thames. It has been built using all of the information that could be found detailing the original, mostly from sketches from the time. You can turn a corner in London and suddenly imagine you are back in the 1500s.

An American actor and director called Sam Wanamaker decided years ago that there should be a permanent celebration of Shakespeare in London, so he started to get the Globe rebuilt. Work on the six metre deep foundations started in 1987 and the building was finally finished in 1997. Unfortunately, Sam died before it was finished but in 1993 the Queen honoured him with an honorary CBE for his hard work on the project.

## GLOBE FACTS:

- As well as putting on plays, the new Globe provides Globe Education for schoolchildren, and the Globe Exhibition.
- Over 750,000 people go there each year!
- The site covers 21000 square metres!
- It has cost £30 million so far and they still want to spend £15 million on making it even better!
- The New Globe lies about 200 yards from what could be the remains of the original, which was found under a house in 1989!
- The Globe Theatre is 33ft high to the eaves (45ft overall).
- 6,000 bundles of Norfolk Water Reed were used on the Globe's roof.
- 36,000 handmade bricks were used.
- 90 tons of lime putty were used for the Tudor brickwork.
- 180 tons of lime plaster went into the outer walls.
- The Globe's pillars, which hold up the roof over the stage, are 28ft high and weigh 3 tons!

# GLOBE RESEARCH SHEET 1

| QUESTION:<br>Shakespeare's Globe, London | |
|---|---|
| At Shakespeare's Globe in London, how many standing tickets are available for each performance? | |
| Who was the architect for Shakespeare's Globe? | |
| And the architect for the original Globe? | |
| Which play was performed at the original Globe in 1599? | |
| Write down 3 facts about The Globe | |
| What is the Supporting Wall? | |
| When was Henry V performed at the 'new' Globe? | |
| Name three areas of the new Globe exhibition. | |
| Who was Edward Alleyn? | |
| In which other countries are there replicas of the Globe? | |

# THE *OTHER* NEW GLOBE

The New Globe in London was so popular that they are building another one in America!

In 1812, America and Britain were at war with each other. In New York Harbour, a military fort, Castle Williams, was built to defend America against the British. It isn't there anymore but there are some remains, which show it had the same shape as Shakespeare's Globe Theatre! Now, a new Globe is being built there to celebrate the culture that America and Britain have in common. They call it "The New Globe For The New World".

This new Globe project is supported by many famous actors and actresses, including Zoe Wanamaker, Sam Wanamaker's daughter!

The New Globe is being built on Governor's Island. In the 19th Century, a fort was built there but no shot was fired from there against the British.

It was then turned into a prison. Criminals were still locked up there well into the 20th century.

The courtyard is exactly the same shape as Shakespeare's Globe.

## TASK:
Use the Internet to find out the answers to the questions on the **Globe Research Sheet.**

Find the information you need at:
**www.newglobe.org**
**www.shakespeares-globe.org**
**www.bbc.co.uk**

# THE GLOBE

## GLOBE THEATRE: Label Descriptions

These are all jumbled up. Work out which description goes with which name, then label the diagram of The Globe with the information that you think is correct.

| | Name | Description |
|---|---|---|
| 1 | | The canopy over the stage, decorated with signs of the zodiac. There was a space above here from which actors could be lowered through a trapdoor as gods or angels. |
| 2 | | Sometimes live music was played here but it was also used for acting as a wall or balcony. |
| 3 | | There were trunks of oak trees put here to hold up The Heavens. The theatre was meant to be like the universe – divided into Heaven, Earth and Hell. |
| 4 | | A thousand Groundlings would stand here to watch the plays. Noisy and smelly! |
| 5 | | Here was the best place to sit if you were a lord or lady because everyone could see you – but your view might not be very good! |
| 6 | | This led down to Hell! It was a room below the stage from where actors playing ghosts, witches and devils could make their entrance. |
| 7 | | Rich playgoers could sit here on cushions. |
| 8 | | An area behind the stage where costumes and props were kept and actors got changed. |

| Name | Number of description |
|---|---|
| The Heavens | |
| The Gentlemen's Rooms | |
| The Trapdoor | |
| The Yard | |
| The Musician's Gallery | |
| The Lord's Rooms | |
| The Tiring House | |
| The Pillars | |

# THE GLOBE

## GLOBE THEATRE: Label Descriptions

Fill in the labels using the descriptions provided.

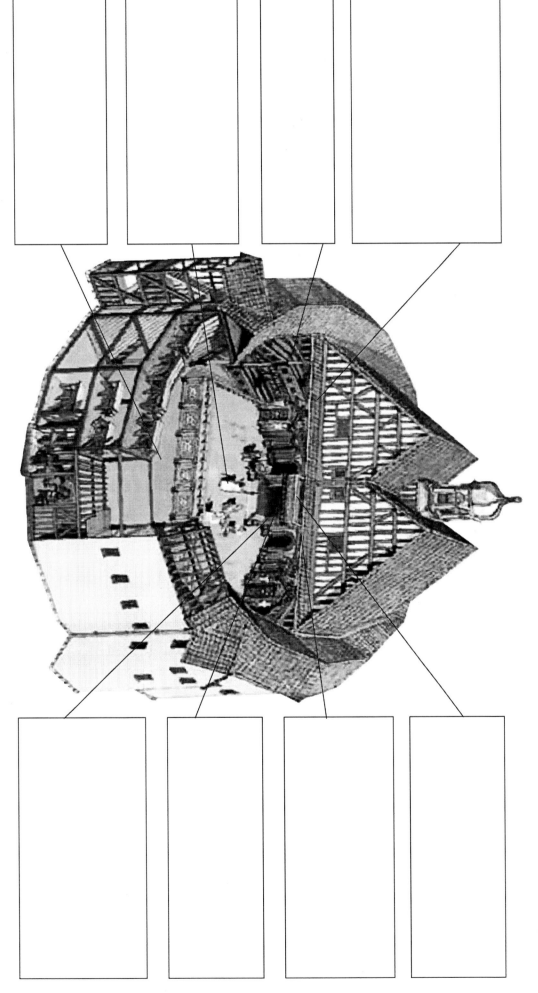

# GLOBE RESEARCH SHEET 2

| QUESTION: <br> **The New Globe, New York** | ANSWER: |
|---|---|
| Name 3 of the actors who are supporting the project. | |
| Find the names of 3 other actors from the list that you have heard of and name a film play or TV show that they have been in. <br><br> OR: <br> If you haven't heard of any of them, find out what the 3 actors you have already named have been in. | |
| One of the actors who supports the project is Zoe Wanamaker. What is her connection to the Globe in London? | |
| **BBC** | |
| What BBC TV comedy features Zoe Wanamaker as the mother of a family? Who does she play in the Harry Potter films? | |
| In which Doctor Who episode did The Doctor and Martha meet William Shakespeare? | |
| In that episode, who played William Shakespeare? | |
| Write down 3 interesting facts about this episode of Doctor Who. | |

# HENRY V TIMELINE

| Date | Key events during the reign of Henry V |
|------|----------------------------------------|
| 1413 | Henry becomes king upon the death of his father, Henry IV. |
| 1415 | Henry stops the plot to replace him on the throne with his cousin. He renews the war against France, captures Harfleur and wins the Battle of Agincourt (October 25th). |
| 1416 | Death of Owain Glyndwr. Henry makes a pilgrimage to St Winifrede's Well in Somerset. |
| 1417 | Henry V is victorious at the Battle of Caen. He takes Pontoise. |
| 1418 | The English army takes Louviers and Compiegne. The Siege of Rouen begins. |
| 1419 | The long siege of Rouen ends. Henry starves the inhabitants into submission. |
| 1420 | Henry becomes Regent of France and heir to the French King Charles VI, under the Treaty of Troyes. Henry marries Katherine. Katherine goes on to found the Tudor Dynasty in England. |
| 1421 | Birth of Prince Henry, later Henry VI. |
| 1422 | Henry V dies at Vincennes in France of dysentery, before he can succeed to the French throne. |

## HENRY V FACTS:

**BORN:** August 9th 1387, Monmouth.

**PARENTS:** Henry IV and Mary de Bohun.

**ASCENDED THE THRONE:** March 20th 1413.

**CROWNED:** April 9th 1413, Westminster Abbey.

**TITLES:** King of England, Duke of Normandy (from 1417), Regent of France (1420).

**MARRIED:** Katherine de Valois, daughter of Charles VI of France (1420).

**CHILDREN:** One son, the future Henry VI.

**DIED:** Vincennes, August 31st 1422.

**BURIED:** Westminster Abbey.

# HENRY RULES OK!

### Henry V 1413-1422

In the years before Henry V became king, there were many wars fought over who should rule the country. Although his father, Henry IV, had control of the throne, Henry V needed to be a strong leader to make sure that nobody tried to replace him. England had been at war for many years with France, and sometimes also with Scotland and Wales. This was before England, Scotland and Wales became one nation as Britain.

Henry V is sometimes described as a great warrior king. He was born in 1386 or 1387, and became king when his father died in 1413.

### What made Henry a warrior king?

- When he was still a prince, he helped his father to fight Owain Glyndwr in Wales. Owain was a Welsh nobleman who did not like being ruled so strictly by England.
- When he became king, he knew that some of his dukes and barons wanted to fight each other. Some of them even wanted to fight him. In 1415, some of them tried to replace Henry with the Earl of March. He managed to defeat them. To make sure it didn't happen again, he got them all together to fight France instead.
- Between 1415 and 1420, Henry sent England to war with France. His first victory was the Battle of Agincourt in 1415. It took four years for the English to reach Paris in 1419, but when they did, the French surrendered. Henry had won!
- As part of the peace agreement with France, Henry married the French Princess Katherine. One day, he hoped to become King of France as well as England.
- He planned to go to war in Jerusalem next, but instead he suddenly died of dysentery in 1422. Many people say he died on the toilet!

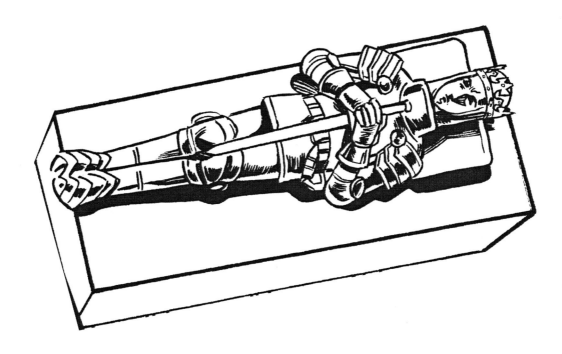

# HENRY V - THE STORY

The play is set in England in the fifteenth century. The young Henry V has just become king, and not everyone is happy about it. Several bitter civil wars have affected the country. The Chorus tells us about these events at the start. Henry used to hang around with thieves and drunkards when he was younger. In order to gain the respect of the country, he needs to put all of that behind him. The Archbishop of Canterbury and Ely encourage Henry V to go to war with France to claim the throne. They base this on his distant roots in the French royal family and some very old laws about land ownership. An ambassador from the French Prince (the Dauphin) brings a case of tennis balls to mock Henry V. He responds by promising to attack France.

Pistol, Bardolph and Nym used to be Henry's friends but they are common men and criminals. As they prepare for the war, they talk about the death of Falstaff, an elderly knight who was once Henry's closest friend. When he became king, Henry rejected all of his old friends but they are still willing to fight for him in France.

Before he leaves for France, Henry finds out that Richard Earl of Cambridge, Henry Lord Scroop of Masham, and Sir Thomas Grey, knight of Northumberland have been paid by the French to murder him. He tricks them into admitting it, and then has them executed, even though they ask for mercy.

In France, Henry's army struggle across the country but manage to defeat the town of Harfleur, where Henry gives a brilliant speech that encourages his men to fight on. Although he has been thinking of trying for peace, the French King is persuaded to fight Henry's army, but he won't let his son, The Dauphin, fight as well.

Bardolph steals money from a church so Henry has him executed. The climax of the war comes at the famous Battle of Agincourt, at which the English are outnumbered by the French five to one. The night before the battle, King Henry disguises himself as a common soldier and talks to many of the soldiers in his camp, learning who they are and what they think of the battle in which they have been told to fight. He argues with some of them about whose fault it is if they die in battle for the king. When he is by himself, he feels the pressure of his responsibilities as king and longs to be a normal man. In the morning, he prays to God and gives a powerful, inspiring speech to his soldiers. In battle, Pistol captures a Frenchman. The Earl of Suffolk and Edward the Duke of York both die in battle. The French, losing the battle, kill all of the boys and servants in the English camp. This is against the rules of war. In retaliation, Henry V has all of the French prisoners killed. The English win the battle, and the French surrender. According to the story, only a few dozen English men die, but 10,000 French men are killed.

A little later, the English and French work out a peace agreement. Part of this involves Henry marrying Katherine, the French King's daughter. He tries hard to persuade her to marry him, and eventually the marriage is agreed. The two royal families are united and the play ends on the plans for marriage, that ensures that Henry's son becomes the King of France.

# HENRY V - THE STORY

## TEST YOURSELF

1. Name all four of Henry's friends from when he was younger.

2. Which friend does he have executed and what was his crime?

3. Which friend dies before they go to France?

4. How does Henry manage to defeat the town of Harfleur?

5. What does Henry do on the evening before the Battle of Agincourt?

6. Who are killed by the French in battle?

7. Why does Henry have all the French prisoners killed?

8. How many French soldiers are killed in battle?

9. Who does Henry ask to marry him at the end of the play?

10. Which countries will Henry VI rule?

# HENRY V - THE STORY

## DISCUSSIONS:

Go online, or use reference books to find out more about the following:

Did you see any mention of archers in the play?

Why was that?

Did you think any parts of the play were "made up" by William Shakespeare?

What would make him embroider or change facts?

Do royal titles and lands still pass from father to son?

What does "civil war" mean?

Did Henry have a good claim to the throne of England?

Katherine (the wife of Henry V) went on to become the grandmother of a king. Who was he?

Can you find out how long the battle lasted?

## ACTIVITIES:

Write a speech for Henry V in the style of William Shakespeare.
Write a newspaper article about the Battle of Agincourt.
Pick a headline, use interviews with witnesses, draw maps and diagrams.

# FAMILY TREE

Look at the Family Tree on the next page and answer the questions below.

1. What are the titles of Henry V's two brothers?

2. How is the Duke of Exeter related to Henry V?

3. What is the name of Henry V's wife?

4. After Henry V gets married, who is his brother-in-law?

5. Which two women in the family tree have similar names?

6. Explain in what way they are related to Henry V.

7. Which of Henry's relatives are not in the play?

# FAMILY TREE

## Key to Roman Numerals:

1 = I
2 = II
3 = III
4 = IV
5 = V
6 = VI
7 = VII
8 = VIII
9 = IX
10 = X

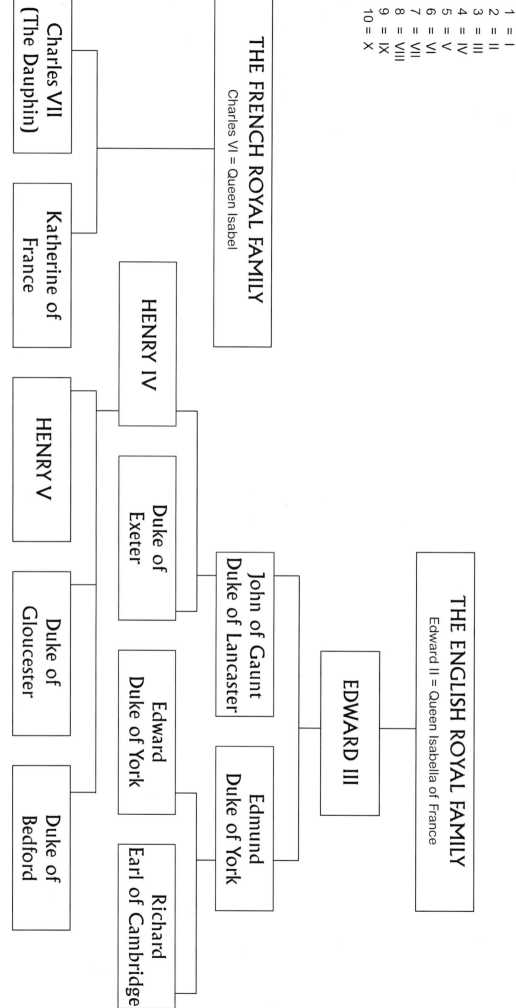

**THE FRENCH ROYAL FAMILY**
Charles VI = Queen Isabel

Charles VII (The Dauphin)

Katherine of France

HENRY IV

HENRY V

Duke of Exeter

Duke of Gloucester

John of Gaunt Duke of Lancaster

Edward Duke of York

Duke of Bedford

Edmund Duke of York

Richard Earl of Cambridge

EDWARD III

**THE ENGLISH ROYAL FAMILY**
Edward II = Queen Isabella of France

Please note: This family tree does not show every member of the families.

22

# THE BATTLE OF AGINCOURT

Shakespeare shows us that Henry begins his attack on France after the Dauphin insults him. However, in the same scene, the Archbishop of Canterbury and the Bishop of Ely spend a long time persuading Henry to claim the throne of France as his own. This is mainly to take Henry's mind away from a tax he plans which would harm the pockets of the church! If successful in his claim, he would be King of France as well as King of England. Shakespeare says that the French King (Charles VI) rejected Henry's claim to the French throne on the basis of Salic law's inheritance rules. Basically it says that the male line will inherit and that daughters of Kings do not count in succession plans.

### The Salic Law

The first thing to remember is that the French royal family and the English royal family at this point in history were related, and there were always arguments going on about who should rule France. The Salic Law is a law that was used in France at the time that stopped women from inheriting land and titles. Henry's great-grandfather was Edward III, whose mother was Queen Isabella of France (see the Family Tree). So, Henry thought that Edward III should have become King of France and decided to take the crown for himself. However, because the Salic Law said that Queen Isabella wasn't entitled to anything, the French said that Henry was wrong. They end up going to war over it!

### The Battle of Agincourt

The battle was part of what we call The Hundred Years' War between England and France. It happened on St Crispin's Day, 25th October 1415. Henry refers to this in his big speech in Act 4 scene 3. The battle is interesting as Henry's army won mainly because of the English longbow. The English archers surrounded the French and they had little chance because the arrows could travel a long distance. The English also drove pointed wooden stakes into the ground at an angle to stop the French cavalry (men on horses) from reaching them. Any French horse unlucky enough to get close would be impaled on a pointed stick!

| **Location:** Agincourt, France | |
|---|---|
| **Result:** Decisive English victory | |
| **Combatants:** | |
| Kingdom of England | Kingdom of France |
| **Commanders:** | |
| Henry V of England | Charles d'Albret of France |
| **Strength:** | |
| About 6,000 (but historians still argue about this) | Between 20,000 and 30,000 (and they argue about this figure too!) |
| **Casualties:** | |
| Around 100-250 Casualties | Around 6,000 Casualties |

# THE BATTLE OF AGINCOURT
## (PART TWO)

## WORKSHEET

**What do you think?**
Was Henry right or wrong to invade France on the basis that the Salic Law was wrong?

**How long was the Hundred Years' War?**

**When did it start, and who started it?**

**Where was the last stronghold of the English in France?**

**When was it surrendered?**

**Which famous Frenchwoman led the French armies to victory at Orleans?**

## FURTHER RESEARCH:

Get to your computer and look at the following internet websites:
**www.geocities.com/beckster05/Agincourt/AgMain.html**
**www.aginc.net/battle/battle-map.htm**

## TASKS:

From website 1 (above) make notes about the battle.
Copy or print out the map from the website. Draw and colour your own version of the map.
Write on the map your own description of what is happening. Use arrows to point to where action is taking place.

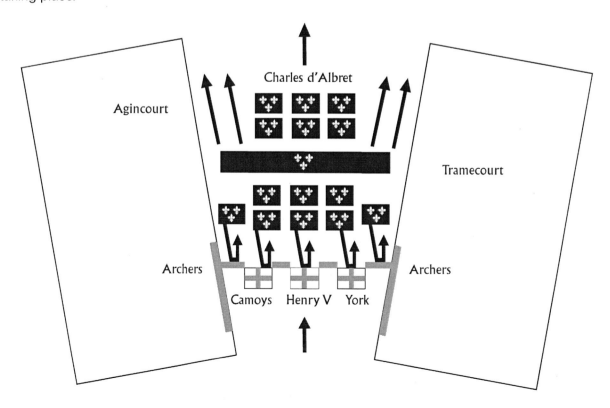

# THE LONGBOW

| Date | Timeline of the Longbow |
|---|---|
| 50,000BC | Arrowheads found in Tunisia, Algeria and Morocco |
| Circa 3,000BC | Longbow first appears in Europe |
| Circa 2,690BC | Evidence of longbow being used in Somerset, England |
| 950AD | Historical evidence of crossbows in France |
| 1066 | Battle of Hastings |
| 1100's | Henry I introduces law that meant any archer was freed if he killed another archer whilst practising |
| Circa 1300 | Edward I bans all sports other than archery on Sundays |
| 1340 | Start of The One Hundred Years War |
| 1346 | Crécy |
| 1356 | Poitiers |
| 1363 | All Englishmen ordered to practice archery on Sunday and holidays |
| 1377 | First mention of Robyn Hode in the poem Piers Plowman written by William Langland |
| 1414 | Agincourt |
| 1453 | English archers killed by cannon and lances attacking French artillery position at Castillon, the last battle of The One Hundred Years War |
| 1472 | English ships ordered to import wood needed to make bows |
| 1508 | To increase use of longbows, crossbows are banned in England |
| 1644 | Tippermuir - Last battle involving the longbow |
| 17th Century | Muskets become more popular |

## TASK:

Research the longbow using sites like:

**www.historylearningsite.co.uk/longbow.htm**

**http://en.wikipedia.org/wiki/Longbow**

## QUESTIONS:

1. How long was an average Longbow?
2. Name three woods that a longbow can be made from.
3. How many pieces of wood are used in a 'self-bow'?
4. Name three major battles between England and France where the longbow was used.
5. What woods were arrows usually made from?
6. What was the maximum range of a longbow?

# HENRY: FOLLOW THE LEADER

## WORKSHEET 1

Henry (nicknamed Harry) is the central character in Henry V. At the beginning of the play, he has only been King for a short amount of time. He is very young and many people do not think he is up to the job of being a leader. The French Dauphin thinks he is just a boy. The Archbishop of Canterbury and the Bishop of Ely aren't sure that he will support the Church yet, so they persuade him to go to war against France in order to ensure his support.

**Is Henry a good leader?**

To answer this question, first think about the following then discuss your answers in a group.

| What do you think are the qualities of a good leader? |
|---|
|  |

Name at least five people who you think are good leaders.

| Name of person. | Why is he or she a good leader? |
|---|---|
|  |  |

| Do you think Henry is a good leader? Give at least one reason. | Which qualities of a good leader does Henry have? |
|---|---|
|  |  |

# HENRY: FOLLOW THE LEADER

## WORKSHEET 2

The Elizabethans had their own ideas about what makes a perfect leader or king.
Compare them to your own ideas and see which you agree with. If you disagree with any of them, think about what your reasons are and discuss this with your group. You might not all agree!

| What the Elizabethans thought made a good leader. | What do you think? Tick to agree or disagree. | | Write your reasons in this column. |
|---|---|---|---|
| | Agree | Disagree | |
| The King must show that he is Christian and support the Christian Church. | | | |
| The King must know a lot about theology (religion). | | | |
| The King must show mercy and never take personal revenge. | | | |
| The King must be very self-controlled and not lose his temper. | | | |
| He should take counsel (advice) from wise men. | | | |
| He should be friendly with the common people but not let it affect his job as King. | | | |
| He must seek to defend and protect the state (his country). | | | |
| He should get rid of bad influences around him – e.g. people who are unhelpful or flatter (suck up to) him too much. | | | |
| He should be concerned about how war will affect his people and his country. | | | |
| He should be married. | | | |

## DISCUSSION:

1.   Which one of these qualities is the most important? Why?
2.   Which one(s) would you get rid of? Why?

# HENRY: FOLLOW THE LEADER

## WORKSHEET 3

Look again at the list. In the play, Henry shows some of these qualities, but sometimes he doesn't. How many of these 'rules' does he break?

| The qualities that Henry should have. | Does Henry show these qualities? Tick yes or no. | | Write your reasons in this column. Explain what Henry does or says. |
|---|---|---|---|
| | Yes | No | |
| The King must show that he is Christian and support the Christian Church. | | | |
| The King must know a lot about theology (religion). | | | |
| The King must show mercy and never take personal revenge. | | | |
| The King must be very self-controlled and not lose his temper. | | | |
| He should take counsel (advice) from wise men. | | | |
| He should be friendly with the common people but not let it affect his job as King. | | | |
| He must seek to defend and protect the state (his country). | | | |
| He should get rid of bad influences around him – e.g. people who are unhelpful or flatter (suck up to) him too much. | | | |
| He should be concerned about how war will affect his people and his country. | | | |
| He should be married. | | | |

# EXTENSION:

Use another copy of this sheet to look at the qualities of a famous leader e.g. the Prime Minister or a famous football manager. How many of these qualities should still apply to leaders today?

# ENGLISH ROYAL CHARACTERS: DUKES AND EARLS

Henry is surrounded by a number of characters who offer him advice and who lead his men into battle. These are all Dukes or Earls, which are hereditary titles, and most of them are related to the King. We are not told their everyday names, just their titles. This is the same today, where Dukes and Earls are often cousins or other relatives of the Royal Family. Even Prince Charles is also the Duke of Cornwall!

The Earls are Salisbury, Earl of Westmoreland, Earl of Warwick.
The Duke of Gloucester and Duke of Bedford are Henry's brothers.
The Duke of York is Henry's cousin.
The Duke of Exeter is Henry's uncle, and plays an important role in the play.

## TASKS:

| Look at Act 2 scene 2. What does Exeter do in this scene? |
|---|
|  |

Here is Exeter's speech from Act 2 scene 4. He is telling the French King what Henry will do if the French do not surrender.

| Underline the words that are about suffering, violence and pain. | |
|---|---|
| Bloody constraint; for if you hide the crown<br>Even in your hearts, there will he rake for it:<br>Therefore in fierce tempest is he coming,<br>In thunder and in earthquake, like a Jove,<br>That, if requiring fail, he will compel;<br>And bids you, in the bowels of the Lord,<br>Deliver up the crown, and to take mercy<br>On the poor souls for whom this hungry war<br>Opens his vasty jaws; and on your head<br>Turning the widows' tears, the orphans' cries<br>The dead men's blood, the pining maidens groans,<br>For husbands, fathers and betrothed lovers,<br>That shall be swallow'd in this controversy.<br>This is his claim, his threat'ning, and my message; | **Write down a simile from the speech:**<br><br><br><br>**Write down three metaphors from the speech:** |

| Describe in your own words what Exeter is threatening that Henry will do: |
|---|
|  |

# THE ARCHBISHOP OF CANTERBURY AND THE BISHOP OF ELY

The Archbishop of Canterbury and The Bishop of Ely represent the English Church, which was a very powerful organisation in Henry's day. They only appear at the beginning of the play, as their role in the drama is to provide a reason for Henry to invade France. They also describe Henry before he appears on stage, so they tell us what he is like before we meet him. This makes us look forward to seeing him to find out for ourselves.

## TASK:

Look at how Canterbury and Ely describe Henry in Act 1 scene 1.

**Underline or highlight words that describe what he is like now.**
**In a different colour, underline words that describe what he used to be like before he became King.**

| | |
|---|---|
| **CANTERBURY:**<br>The breath no sooner left his father's body,<br>But that his wildness, mortifi'd in him,<br>Seem'd to die too…<br>Hear him debate of Common-wealth affairs;<br>You would say, it hath been all in all his study:<br>List his discourse of war; and you shall hear<br>A fearful battle render'd you in music.<br>Turn him to any cause of policy,<br>The Gordian Knot of it he will unloose…<br>Which is a wonder how his Grace should glean it,<br>Since his addiction was to courses vain,<br>His companies unletter'd, rude, and shallow,<br>His hours fill'd up with riots, banquets, sports;<br>And never noted in him any study,<br>Any retirement, any sequestration,<br>From open haunts and popularity.<br><br>**ELY:**<br>The strawberry grows underneath the nettle,<br>And wholesome berries thrive and ripen best,<br>Neighbour'd by fruit of baser quality:<br>And so the Prince obscur'd his contemplation<br>Under the veil of wildness, which (no doubt)<br>Grew like the summer grass, fastest by night,<br>Unseen, yet crescive in his faculty. | Describe in your own words the differences between the way Henry was when he was a young prince and what he is like now. Complete your answer below.<br><br>When Henry was young, he…<br><br><br><br><br><br>As a King, Henry is… |

## RESEARCH AND QUESTIONS:

Canterbury compares Henry to **Alexander The Great** when he refers to the Gordian Knot.
Use the internet or your school library to find out the following:

1. **Who was Alexander the Great and what did he do to become famous?**
2. **What was the Gordian Knot and what did it have to do with Alexander?**
3. **What does Canterbury mean when he mentions the Gordian Knot in his description of Henry?**
4. **What does Ely mean when he compares Henry to a strawberry growing "underneath the nettle"?**

# THE ARCHBISHOP OF CANTERBURY
# AND THE BISHOP OF ELY

## DISCUSSION:

Are the Archbishop of Canterbury and The Bishop of Ely acting the way you would expect religious men to?

How concerned are they with their own wealth and status?

What was their main reason for encouraging Henry to go to war against France?

What would have happened if the churchmen had asked Henry not to go to war?

Set up an interview with one of the class playing the Archbishop, and another being a journalist interviewing him. Perhaps on TV?

The interview should ask strong questions about war and the 10 commandments, and how a religious man could encourage bloodshed.

Prepare the questions in advance, and let the 'Archbishop' have time to prepare answers!!

The rest of the class (the audience) should keep a tally of who scores the most points!

# THE TRAITORS

The traitors who plot against Henry accept money from the French in order to betray him. Shakespeare doesn't explain what their exact plans are, only that they are planning to kill him somehow. The Chorus tells us that Henry finds out and, in Act 2 scene 2, he traps them into admitting their guilt. We don't get much of an idea of them as characters, but when they are found out they beg for mercy and apologise.

In Act 2 scene 2, the three men the Earl of Cambridge, Lord Scroop of Masham, and Sir Thomas Grey, Knight of Northumberland, are brought to Henry. He knows that they have betrayed him. He starts by asking them what they think of the intention to invade France. They flatter him and agree it is a good idea. He then tells them about a man who criticised him when drunk, who he has in jail. He asks them what he should do with him. They all say that they should punish him by execution instead of letting him go. When Henry reveals that he knows what they have done, they can see that he has trapped them. If the prisoner had to die to set an example, then so should they.

# TASK 1:

Imagine you are directing the scene where Henry traps the traitors. Write down the directions that you would give the actors. Explain how you want them to move, how to react to particular lines etc. Should they show anger? Or surprise? Or fear? How?

| Act 2 Scene 2 | Stage Directions |
|---|---|
| **KING HENRY V**<br>Now sits the wind fair, and we will aboard.<br>My Lord of Cambridge, and my kind Lord of Masham,<br>And you, my gentle knight, give me your thoughts:<br>Think you not that the powers we bear with us<br>Will cut their passage through the force of France,<br>Doing the execution and the act<br>For which we have in head assembled them?<br><br>**SCROOP**<br>No doubt, my liege, if each man do his best.<br><br>**KING HENRY V**<br>I doubt not that; since we are well persuaded<br>We carry not a heart with us from hence<br>That grows not in a fair consent with ours,<br>Nor leave not one behind that doth not wish<br>Success and conquest to attend on us.<br><br>**CAMBRIDGE**<br>Never was monarch better fear'd and loved<br>Than is your majesty: there's not, I think, a subject<br>That sits in heart-grief and uneasiness<br>Under the sweet shade of your government.<br><br>**GREY**<br>True: those that were your father's enemies<br>Have steep'd their galls in honey and do serve you<br>With hearts create of duty and of zeal. | |

| Act 2 Scene 2 | Stage Directions |
|---|---|
| **KING HENRY V**<br>…Uncle of Exeter,<br>Enlarge the man committed yesterday,<br>That rail'd against our person: we consider<br>it was excess of wine that set him on;<br>And on his more advice we pardon him.<br><br>**SCROOP**<br>That's mercy, but too much security:<br>Let him be punish'd, sovereign, lest example<br>Breed, by his sufferance, more of such a kind.<br><br>**KING HENRY V**<br>O, let us yet be merciful.<br><br>**CAMBRIDGE**<br>So may your highness, and yet punish too.<br><br>**GREY**<br>Sir, You show great mercy, if you give him life,<br>After the taste of much correction.<br><br>**KING HENRY V**<br>Alas, your too much love and care of me<br>Are heavy orisons 'gainst this poor wretch!<br>If little faults, proceeding on distemper,<br>Shall not be wink'd at, how shall we stretch our eye<br>When capital crimes, chew'd, swallow'd and digested,<br>Appear before us? We'll yet enlarge that man,<br>Though Cambridge, Scroop and Grey, in their dear care<br>And tender preservation of our person,<br>Would have him punished.<br>And now to our French causes: Who are the<br>late commissioners?<br><br>**CAMBRIDGE**<br>I one, my lord:Your highness bade me ask for it to-day.<br><br>**SCROOP**<br>So did you me, my liege.<br><br>**GREY**<br>And I, my royal sovereign.<br><br>**KING HENRY V**<br>Then, Richard Earl of Cambridge, there is yours;<br>There yours, Lord Scroop of Masham; and, sir knight,<br>Grey of Northumberland, this same is yours:<br>Read them; and know, I know your worthiness. |  |

| Act 2 Scene 2 | Stage Directions |
|---|---|
| **KING HENRY V**<br>...Why, how now, gentlemen!<br>What see you in those papers that you lose<br>So much complexion? Look ye, how they change!<br>Their cheeks are paper. Why, what read you there<br>That hath so cowarded and chased your blood<br>Out of appearance?<br><br>**CAMBRIDGE**<br>I do confess my fault;<br>And do submit me to your highness' mercy.<br><br>**GREY, SCROOP**<br>To which we all appeal.<br><br>**KING HENRY V**<br>The mercy that was quick in us but late,<br>By your own counsel is suppress'd and kill'd:<br>You must not dare, for shame, to talk of mercy;<br>For your own reasons turn into your bosoms,<br>As dogs upon their masters, worrying you.<br>See you, my princes, and my noble peers,<br>These English monsters!...<br><br>**EXETER**<br>I arrest thee of high treason, by the name of<br>Richard Earl of Cambridge.<br>I arrest thee of high treason, by the name of<br>Henry Lord Scroop of Masham.<br>I arrest thee of high treason, by the name of<br>Thomas Grey, knight, of Northumberland.<br><br>**SCROOP**<br>Our purposes God justly hath discover'd;<br>And I repent my fault more than my death;<br>Which I beseech your highness to forgive,<br>Although my body pay the price of it.<br><br>**CAMBRIDGE**<br>For me, the gold of France did not seduce;<br>Although I did admit it as a motive<br>The sooner to effect what I intended:<br>But God be thanked for prevention;<br>Which I in sufferance heartily will rejoice,<br>Beseeching God and you to pardon me.<br><br>**GREY**<br>Never did faithful subject more rejoice<br>At the discovery of most dangerous treason<br>Than I do at this hour joy o'er myself.<br>Prevented from a damned enterprise:<br>My fault, but not my body, pardon, sovereign. | |

# TASK 2:

In groups of 5, act out the above scene using your stage directions. Mime the actions without saying any of the words. See if you can show the characters' emotions without using the script.

# THE SOLDIERS IN THE KING'S ARMY

The soldiers **Bates, Court** and **Williams** show us what the common man thinks of Henry's war against France. When Henry goes into the soldiers' camp in disguise in Act 4 scene 1, he argues with Bates and Williams about whether the king is to blame if they die in battle.

| The Argument | What does this mean? |
|---|---|
| **HENRY:**<br>…methinks I could not die anywhere so contented, as in the King's company; his cause being just, and his quarrel honourable. | |
| **BATES:**<br>…if his (Henry's) cause be wrong, our obedience to the King wipes the crime of it out of us. | |
| **WILLIAMS:**<br>But if the cause be not good, the King himself hath a heavy reckoning to make, when all those legs, and arms, and heads, chopped off in a battle, shall join together at the latter day… Now, if these men do not die well, it will be a black matter for the King, that led them to it; whom to disobey, were against all proportion of subjection. | |
| **HENRY:**<br>So, if a son that is by his father sent about merchandise, do sinfully miscarry upon the sea; the imputation of his wickedness, by your rule, should be imposed upon his father that sent him: or if a servant, under his master's command, transporting a sum of money, be assail'd by robbers, and die… you may call the business of the master the author of the servant's damnation: but this is not so: the King is not bound to answer the particular endings of his soldiers, the father of his son, nor the master of his servant; for they purpose not their death when they purpose their services. | |
| **WILLIAMS:**<br>'Tis certain, every man that dies ill, the ill upon his own head, the King is not to answer it. | |
| **Notes:**<br>Henry's "cause" means his reason for going to war.<br>The "latter day" refers to 'Judgement Day', when, according to Christian belief, everyone will rise from the dead to be judged as a good or bad person by God. | |

# TASK:

On a separate piece of paper, write four paragraphs in your own words:

Paragraph 1:    Explain what Bates says about Henry's cause.

Paragraph 2:    Explain what Williams says about Henry's cause.

Paragraph 3:    Explain how Henry argues that it is not the King's fault if one of his soldiers dies.

Paragraph 4:    Explain what you think. Do you think Henry's reason for going to war is a good one (his cause is just)?

# THE CAPTAINS IN THE KING'S ARMY

The Captains are almost an old joke, each one representing a different country.

| | |
|---|---|
| Sir Thomas Erpingham | English |
| Gower | English |
| Fluellen | Welsh |
| Macmorris | Irish |
| Jamy | Scottish |

Strangely, although Gower is in Wales, the character Gower is English! Also, 'Mac' sounds Scottish but Macmorris is Irish! Fluellen is definitely Welsh. The Welsh spelling of his name would be 'Llewelyn'.

In Fluellen's speech, many words are spelt in an unusual way. It is unclear whether Shakespeare thought all Welshmen spoke this way or just Fluellen, but he uses a 'p' sound instead of 'b' in many words. He is full of opinions although he admires Henry. When Henry tricks him into fighting Williams with the glove, Henry seems only to be doing it out of fun or to test their loyalty – which is a little unfair!

## TASK:

Look at Act 4 scene 7, where Fluellen has lots to say. Find as many words as you can that he seems to pronounce differently from everybody else. Write them down and then write down the correct spelling.

| Fluellen's words | Correct spelling |
|---|---|
| e.g. porn | born |
| | |

# PISTOL, NYM AND BARDOLPH

Shakespeare's audiences would already know Pistol, Nym, Bardolph and Hostess Quickly from the earlier history plays, Henry IV Parts One and Two. In a way, Henry V was a sequel to those other plays. This is common in films today – e.g. Spider-Man 2 is a sequel to Spider-Man. The Hostess runs the Boar's Head Tavern, which is where Henry, as Prince Hal, used to drink with Falstaff and the cowardly rogues Pistol, Nym and Bardolph.

## QUESTIONS:

Write your answers on a separate sheet of paper.

### Act 2 scene 1

1.     What does Nym say "will toast cheese"? What does he mean?
2.     Why does Nym want to fight Pistol?
3.     Write down examples of how the characters argue and swear at each other.

### Act 2 scene 3

4.     Why are Pistol, Nym and Bardolph so sad in this scene?
5.     How does the Hostess describe Falstaff's death?
6.     From what they say, describe what you think Falstaff was like.

### Act 3 scene 2

7.     Look at what the Boy says about Pistol, Nym and Bardolph. Write in your own words what he says about them.
8.     Do you think the Boy is right to decide to get away from them? Explain your answer.

### Act 3 scene 6

9.     Why does Pistol say "Fortune is Bardolph's foe, and frowns on him"?
       (Remember: 'fortune' is another word for 'luck' and
       'foe' means 'enemy')
10.    What does Pistol mean when he says to Fluellen
       "Speak Captain for his life, and I will thee requite"?
11.    What is Fluellen's answer?

### Act 4 scenes 1 and 4

12.    In scene 1, what message does Pistol
       ask Henry to give Fluellen when
       he meets him in disguise?
13.    In scene 4, what does Pistol do?
       Explain why this is scene is funny.

# THE FRENCH COURT

The French characters are mainly made up of nobles who advise the French King Charles VI and the Dauphin. There is also Montjoy the Herald, whose job it is to take messages to the English. And of course there is Princess Katherine, her mother Queen Isabel, and Katherine's maid Alice.

**The French Nobles:**
King Charles
The Dauphin
Dukes of Burgundy, Orleans and
Bourbon
The Constable
Lords Rambures and Grandpré

# QUESTIONS:
Write your answers on a separate sheet of paper.

**Act 2 scene 4**
1.      Who sent Henry "this tun of treasure" in Act 1 and what did it contain?
2.      Who tells the Dauphin that he is mistaken about Henry's personality?
3.      Who wants more time to think about Exeter's message from Henry?
4.      How does the Dauphin describe the way that England is ruled?
5.      Which five characters are sent by King Charles to strengthen the French defences to be ready for the English invasion?

**Katherine**
Katherine does not appear until Act 3 scene 4, where she is being taught English quite badly by Alice.
1.      Write down three English words that she learns.
2.      Write down two English words that she pronounces incorrectly.
3.      Compare this to the way she appears in Act 5 scene 2. In what ways has her English improved?
4.      Here are three sentences that Katherine says. Rewrite them in standard English:

| |
|---|
| Is it possible dat I sould love de enemy of France? |
| |
| Dat is not be de fashon pour les Ladies of France. |
| |
| I cannot tell wat is dat. |
| |

# KEY WORDS AND IMAGERY

## WORKSHEET 1

In Shakespeare's plays, speeches by his main characters were good opportunities for him to 'show off' with language. He created strong images in speeches and soliloquies, using metaphor and simile. Shakespeare used many different literary techniques, but here let's focus on metaphor and simile.

## DEFINITIONS:

### Soliloquy

This is when a character in a play is alone on the stage and makes a speech where he or she talks about their feelings and concerns. It is a way for the audience to know what a character is thinking and see a side of the character that he or she keeps private. Other characters cannot hear them, only the audience. Think of it as 'thinking aloud'. Henry does this in Act 4 scene 1 (the "Upon the King…" speech).

### Simile

A simile is a figure of speech where the writer compares two things that seem at first to be nothing like each other. A simile always uses the words 'like' or 'as'.
For example:

"She is **as** beautiful **as** a rose"          "He was so angry that he exploded **like** a volcano"
"You're **as** greedy **as** a pig"          "You were **like** an angel to me"

### Metaphor

A metaphor compares two things in a similar way to a simile, except it gives a description to something that at first doesn't seem to fit but is actually saying something about the qualities of what it is describing. Look for the use of 'is' or 'was' and 'are' or 'were' instead of 'like' or 'as'.
For example:

"She **is** a beautiful rose"          "He **was** an exploding volcano!"
"You **are** a greedy pig!"          "You **were** an angel to me"

## TASK:

Pick any object in the room. Think of an adjective to describe it. Think of another thing that you could describe with the same adjective. Fill in the gaps below to create a simile. Look at the example first.

| The | cloud | is | white | like | fresh snow. |
|-----|-------|-----|-------|------|-------------|
| The |       | is |       | like |             |

Now turn it into a metaphor, as in the example. Feel free to expand on it.

| The | cloud is | fresh snow in the sky. |
|-----|----------|------------------------|
| The |          |                        |

# IMAGERY IN HENRY'S SPEECHES

## WORKSHEET 2

Henry makes two important speeches to his men in Act 3 scene 1 and Act 4 scene 3. His soliloquy appears in Act 4 scene 1. Re-read the speeches looking for examples of metaphor and simile (hint: one of the speeches doesn't have many!) If possible, underline or highlight them when you find them. Put 'M' or 'S' in the margin next to each one. If you have time, look for other examples of metaphor/simile in the play. Hint: look at what Canterbury and Ely and the Duke of Exeter say about Henry. Discuss this as a group. Have you identified them correctly?

## TASK:

Look again at the following images from the speeches and from other parts of the play.
Explain what Henry is saying to his men.

| Image | M or S | Meaning |
|---|---|---|
| "But when the blast of war blows in our ears, Then imitate the action of the tiger" | | |
| "I see you stand like greyhounds in the slips, Straining upon the start." | | |
| "And gentlemen in England, now a-bed, Shall think themselves accurs'd they were not here; And hold their manhoods cheap" | | |
| "O hard condition, twin-born with greatness, Subject to the breath of every fool". | | |
| "The strawberry grows underneath the nettle, And wholesome berries thrive and ripen best, Neighbour'd by fruit of baser quality" | | |
| "…the Prince obscur'd his contemplation Under the veil of wildness, which (no doubt) Grew like the summer grass, fastest by night, Unseen" | | |
| "…in fierce tempest he is coming, In thunder and in earthquake, like a Jove" | | |
| "An angel is like you Kate, and you are like an angel". | | |

# SHAKESPEARE'S LANGUAGE

Shakespeare wrote his plays differently from the way plays are written today. Many of the lines spoken by characters are in a form of poetry called **blank verse**. Shakespeare wrote Henry V using a mixture of blank verse and prose. The parts of the play that look like poetry are in blank verse.

Shakespeare's version of blank verse usually has ten syllables in each line. Each syllable is like a beat of a drum. Try reading the following lines aloud whilst tapping out the beat with your hand:

| 1 | 2 | 3 | 4 | 5 | 6 | 7 | 8 | 9 | 10 |
|---|---|---|---|---|---|---|---|---|---|
| Once | more | un | to | the | breach | dear | friends, | once | more |
| Or | close | up | the | wall | with | our | Eng | lish | dead. |

Each pair of syllables is called an **iamb**. In each pair, one syllable is stressed and the other is unstressed. Try reading the above lines aloud to see which syllables are stressed. The style of having blank verse with ten syllables per line is called **iambic pentameter**. This gives the words a rhythm that is a bit musical but also sounds like natural speech. The rhythm made it easier for actors to remember and to say aloud, especially as they had to perform in the open air and they didn't have microphones!

# TASKS:

1. Find a speech in the play that is written in blank verse. Divide it into syllables like the example above. Underline the syllables that you think are stressed. Can you explain why particular syllables are stressed?

| 1 | 2 | 3 | 4 | 5 | 6 | 7 | 8 | 9 | 10 |
|---|---|---|---|---|---|---|---|---|---|
|   |   |   |   |   |   |   |   |   |   |
|   |   |   |   |   |   |   |   |   |   |

2. Make up your own conversation or speech using only ten syllables per line. It could be a speech about a topic (e.g. explaining why you think your school should get rid of school uniform) or a conversation where two characters are arguing (e.g. a boy or girl is late home from school and Mum wants an explanation). You could work on your own or in pairs. Try reading it aloud and listen to the rhythm.

3. Look closely at the play. Which characters speak in blank verse? Which characters speak in prose?

4. Usually, Henry speaks in blank verse. Sometimes he speaks in prose. Who is Henry talking to when he speaks prose? In which scene does it happen? Explain why he changes the way he speaks in this scene.

# SHAKESPEARE'S LANGUAGE
## (PART TWO)

Shakespeare invented more than 1,000 words, and rather a lot of new phrases too!
He was by far the most important individual influence on the way the modern English that we speak today was developed.

Writers often invent words, either by creating new forms of existing words or inventing new words outright. This is often because they are unable to find the exact word they require in the existing language.

**Here are just some of the words.**

frugal
palmy
gloomy
gnarled
hurry
impartial
inauspicious
indistinguishable
invulnerable
lapse
laughable
lonely
majestic
misplaced
monumental
multitudinous
obscene
seamy
perusal
pious
premeditated
radiance
reliance
road
sanctimonious

accommodation
aerial
amazement
apostrophe
assassination
auspicious
baseless
bloody
bump
castigate
changeful
generous
submerge
suspicious
countless
courtship
critic
critical
dexterously
dishearten
dislocate
dwindle
eventful
exposure
fitful

# SHAKESPEARE'S LANGUAGE
## (PART TWO)

**And here are some of the phrases:**

"dog will have his day"

"eat out of house and home"

"method in his madness"

"to thine own self be true"

"towering passion"

"the course of true love never did run smooth"

"ministering angel"

"too much of a good thing"

# TASKS:

1.  Can you pick ten of Shakespeare's words, and give their meanings?
2.  Pick another five words, and make sentences that include them.
3.  Write a paragraph using one of Shakespeare's phrases.
4.  Find another phrase coined by Shakespeare that isn't shown here.
5.  Make up a word and phrase of your own, giving meanings for both.

# HOW INSULTING!
# THE SHAKESPEARE ABUSE MATRIX

**Shakespeare** often made up his own words, especially when he wanted to create strong images. Many of these were used by characters to insult each other. Can you work out which words are still used today? Match one word from Column 1 with one word from Column 2 and one from Column 3. Cut them out and shuffle them around. Try different combinations to see who can produce the most offensive insult! Put the word 'thou' (you) at the beginning and you have a sentence.

Words made from putting two words together are called compound words. Can you work out what some of them might mean?

| Column 1:<br>**Adjective** | Column 2:<br>**Compound Adjective** | Column 3:<br>**Nouns and Compound Nouns** |
|---|---|---|
| artless | base-court | apple-john |
| bawdy | bat-fowling | baggage |
| beslubbering | beef-witted | barnacle |
| bootless | beetle-headed | basket-cockle |
| burly-boned | boil-brained | bladder |
| caluminous | brazen-faced | blind-worm |
| churlish | bunch-back'd | boar-pig |
| cockered | clapper-clawed | braggart |
| clouted | clay-brained | bugbear |
| craven | common-kissing | canker-blossom |
| cullionly | crook-pated | clotpole |
| currish | dismal-dreaming | coxcomb |
| dankish | dizzy-eyed | codpiece |
| dissembling | doghearted | cur |
| droning | dread-bolted | death-token |
| errant | earth-vexing | devil-monk |
| fawning | elf-skinned | dewberry |
| fishified | fat-kidneyed | flap-dragon |
| fobbing | fen-sucked | flax-wench |
| frothy | flap-mouthed | flirt-gill |
| fusty | fly-bitten | foot-licker |
| gleeking | folly-fallen | fustilarian |
| goatish | fool-born | giglet |
| gorbellied | full-gorged | gudgeon |
| impertinent | guts-griping | haggard |
| infectious | half-faced | harpy |
| jarring | hasty-witted | hedge-pig |
| loggerheaded | hedge-born | horn-beast |
| lumpish | hell-hated | hugger-mugger |
| mammering | idle-headed | jolt-head |
| mangled | ill-breeding | lewdster |
| misbegotten | ill-nurtured | lout |
| mewling | knotty-pated | malcontent |
| odiferous | leaden-footed | maggot-pie |

| Column 1:<br>Adjective | Column 2:<br>Compound Adjective | Column 3:<br>Nouns and Compound Nouns |
|---|---|---|
| paunchy | lily-livered | malt-worm |
| poisonous | malmsey-nosed | mammet |
| pribbling | milk-livered | measle |
| puking | motley-minded | minnow |
| puny | muddy-mettled | miscreant |
| qualling | onion-eyed | mouldwarp |
| rampallian | pigeon-liver'd | mumble-news |
| rank | plume-plucked | nut-hook |
| reeky | pottle-deep | pigeon-egg |
| roguish | pox-marked | pignut |
| ruttish | reeling-ripe | popinjay |
| saucy | rough-hewn | puttock |
| spleeny | rude-growing | pumpion |
| spongy | rump-fed | rascal |
| surly | scale-sided | ratsbane |
| tottering | scurvy-valiant | scullion |
| unmuzzled | shard-borne | scut |
| unwash'd | sheep-biting | skainsmate |
| venomed | spur-galled | strumpet |
| villainous | swag-bellied | toad |
| warped | tardy-gaited | varlot |
| wart-necked | tickle-brained | vassal |
| wayward | toad-spotted | whey-face |
| weedy | unchin-snouted | wagtail |
| whoreson | weather-bitten | yoke-devil |

# GAME:

Divide the class into two. Line up the two halves facing each other, making Line 1 and Line 2. This may be best done outside! Take turns to shout out words from the list as follows:

1.  The first person in Line 1 calls out a word of his or her choice from Column 1.
2.  The first person in Line 2 has to respond with a word starting with the same letter from Column 2.
3.  The second person in Line 1 then completes the insult with any word from Column 3.
4.  The process starts again with the second person in Line 2, and so on.

**Optional extra rule:**

Everyone must listen and try to avoid repeating words that have already been called out. Anyone who repeats a word is 'out' and has to leave the line. The game continues until only a few people are left or the words have all been used up.

# HENRY V SPELLING JUMBLE - ANAGRAMS

The words below are all names of characters or places in the play. Unscramble the letters and write the correct spelling. Don't peek!

| Jumbled Spelling | Correct Spelling |
|---|---|
| FORE GODS CUTE LUKE | |
| F: THY HITHER FEN | |
| FISH POLE BOY | |
| U HAD PIN | |
| FEAR HURL | |
| CROOL DROPS | |
| CUGO TRAIN | |
| DR. B.P. HALO | |
| CRY! RACE FOR POSH, THIN BUBA! | |
| I HATE RENK | |
| BARF! I GORED CAMEL! | |

# MISSING WORDS

To complete the sentences below, underline the correct word in the box, then write it in the gap.
Be careful – there are some traps in the box!

1.    'Dauphin' is the French word for _____ .

2.    "Once more unto the _____ ."

3.    "But when the blast of war blows in our ears,
      Then imitate the _____ of the _____ "

4.    "The strawberry grows underneath the _____ ,
      And wholesome berries thrive and _____ best,
      Neighbour'd by fruit of baser _____ "

5.    The Duke of Exeter is Henry's _____ .

6.    Henry marries Princess _____ .

7.    The French King thinks that King Henry is _____ and "bred out of
      that _____ strain", meaning that Henry could be as powerful as his ancestor, _____
      Black Prince of _____ .

8.    Henry threatens the governor of _____ that he will see old men "taken by their silver
      _____ and their most reverend _____ dash'd to the walls".

9.    Henry gets Fluellen to wear Williams' _____ in his _____ .

10.   The Battle of _____ was fought on Saint _____ 's Day.

| | | |
|---|---|---|
| beach | dolphin | Harfleur |
| prince | whales | action |
| breach | elephant | Crispian |
| tiger | Alice | attraction |
| Katherine | glove | bloody |
| uncle | nettle | mettle | Edward |
| tripe | Christmas | Harlow |
| ripen | quality | Isabel | qualify |
| heads | breads | brother |
| Argentina | cape | strong |
| Wales | beards | Agincourt |
| cap | Crispin | |

# THE BLACK BOOK

## WORKSHEET 1

When Henry V was king, there were very strict rules about the way that the army should behave. Being a soldier was not a job in the way it is today, and the men in Henry's army were not highly trained. Most of them would have been farmers or common men who volunteered to fight during wartime.

The king created various laws called 'statutes' or 'ordinances'. Many of these gave his soldiers and sailors rules that they had to follow. If a man broke any of the rules he could go to prison or even be sentenced to death!

These laws were published in The Black Book of the Admiralty.

**Some of the laws were:**

1.      First, all manner of men should be obedient to our Lord the King.

2.      No man (unless he be a priest) shall touch the sacrament, upon pain of being drawn and hanged; and no man shall touch the box or vessel which the precious sacrament is in, upon the same pain.

3.      No man shall rob the holy church.

4.      No man shall rob a merchant, victualler, surgeon or barber.

5.      No man shall cry 'havoc' without quarter.

6.      No man shall rob or pillage after peace is proclaimed.

7.      No man shall sell or ransom a prisoner without his captain's permission.

## TASK:

Make a list of any words that you don't know from the laws.
Find out what they mean.
Rewrite the laws in your own words.

# THE BLACK BOOK

## WORKSHEET 2

Compare your version with the one below.

**The laws in modern English:**

1.  Every type of man should do what the King tells him to do.

2.  No man (unless he is a priest) is allowed to touch the bread and wine blessed for the Eucharist ceremony. He can't even touch the box that it is in. If he does, he will be cut open, beheaded and his body divided into four pieces.

3.  No man is allowed to steal from a church.

4.  No man is allowed to steal from a salesman, an innkeeper, a surgeon or a barber. In Henry's time, a barber not only cut hair, but he might also fix broken bones, amputate limbs and pull teeth!

5.  No man is allowed to order soldiers to kill lots of enemies without a very good reason.

6.  No man is allowed to steal from the enemy or damage the enemy's property after peace is announced.

7.  No man is allowed to imprison an enemy soldier and ask for money to return him unless he has permission from his captain.

# THINK:

1.  Do you think any of the rules are unfair? Give reasons to explain your answer.
2.  Why do you think the punishments are so harsh?
3.  Do any characters in the play break any of these rules?
4.  How does Henry punish people who break his rules?

# WHAT HAPPENS NEXT?

## TASK 1:

Look closely at the pictures on each card in the following pages. In the box, write down what you think is happening in each scene. You need to have read the play first!

| Comic Card | WHAT IS HAPPENING? Describe in your own words. Try to explain what is going on in each panel and what characters are saying. Can you remember what happens next? |
|---|---|
| CARD 1 | |
| CARD 2 | |
| CARD 3 | |
| CARD 4 | |

# COMIC CARD 1

## Henry V Act 1 Scene 1

# COMIC CARD 2

## Henry V Act 3 Scene 3

# COMIC CARD 3

Henry V Act 4 Scene 1

# COMIC CARD 4

Henry V Act 5 Scene 2

# WHAT HAPPENS NEXT?

## TASK 2:

Look again at Comic Card 4. Cut out the blank word balloons below and write in them the words that you think that the characters are saying to each other.

**You should:**

- Make sure that the 'tail' of the balloon is pointing at the correct character.
- Make sure that the word balloons follow from left to right so that you can follow the conversation easily.
- When you are sure that you have them in the right place, stick the word balloons to the sheet.

**You could:**

- Write the exact words from the play (this might be difficult to fit in!)
- Write the words in modern English.
- Make up your own words for the characters, but make sure that they are still saying the same sort of thing to each other.

There are more word balloons than you need here. You could draw your own if you prefer.

# HENRY V QUIZ

Write A, B or C in the Answer column.

| No. | Question | Answer |
|---|---|---|
| 1 | Which device did Shakespeare use to introduce each Act?<br>a.    an orchestra<br>b.    a chorus<br>c.    a chorus line | |
| 2 | Canterbury claims that Henry can claim the French throne because of a law that stopped a family's inheritance from being passed on to:<br>a.    children<br>b.    Welsh people<br>c.    women | |
| 3 | What is this law called?<br>a.    The Salic Law<br>b.    The Slavic Law<br>c.    The Saliva Law | |
| 4 | Which three characters plot to kill Henry?<br>a.    Pistol, Nym and Bardolph<br>b.    Earl of Cambridge, The Bishop of Ely and Lord Scroop<br>c.    Earl of Cambridge, Sir Thomas Gray and Lord Scroop | |
| 5 | Who does Henry have executed for stealing from a church?<br>a.    Pistol<br>b.    Lord Scroop<br>c.    Bardolph | |
| 6 | On which day does the Battle of Agincourt take place?<br>a.    St David's Day<br>b.    St Christopher's Day<br>c.    St Crispin's Day | |

| No. | Question | Answer |
|---|---|---|
| 7 | Who does Henry say "come pouring like the tide into a breach" every time the English go to war?<br>a.    The Scottish<br>b.    The Welsh<br>c.    The Irish | |
| 8 | Which of these characters used to be Henry's friends?<br>a.    The Dauphin, The French King and Falstaff<br>b.    Bardolph, Williams and Falstaff<br>c.    Bardolph, Pistol and Falstaff | |
| 9 | Which of Henry's old friends died in his bed, heartbroken that Henry rejected him?<br>a.    Pistol<br>b.    The Duke of York<br>c.    Falstaff | |
| 10 | Do most characters describe Henry as:<br>a.    a perfect Christian ruler<br>b.    a really good tennis player<br>c.    a power-hungry ruler | |
| 11 | To which characters does Henry say the following?<br>"I will weep for thee;<br>For this revolt of thine, methinks, is like<br>Another fall of man."<br>a.    the French royal family<br>b.    the three traitors<br>c.    his soldiers, just before the battle | |
| 12 | What does Bates mean when he says "if his cause be wrong, our obedience to the King wipes the crime of it out of us"?<br>a.    If Henry's war is wrong, we won't be to blame because we're just following orders.<br>b.    If Henry's war is wrong, he'll forgive us for our crimes.<br>c.    If Henry's war is wrong, then we're wrong too and we will be blamed. | |
| | Mark out of 12: | |

# WAR! WHAT IS IT GOOD FOR?

Henry V is a play set during war. Whether it is right to declare war is an important theme in the play, and it is a question that still arises today. For example, when the UK and the USA went to war in Iraq, many people protested that the war was not happening for good reasons.

It also looks at the role of the King as a war leader.

Shakespeare writes about the reasons for war, the heroes of the time, the victims and the impact on all of the people. He shows that although the battles may be heroic, with amazing acts of bravery, it also encourages terrible behaviour from cheats, cowards and thieves.

## GROUP WORK AND DISCUSSION:

1.      In groups, create a Mind Map of all the words and phrases that you can think of that are to do with war.

2.      Then, divide them into 'negative' and 'positive' halves. Does every group have the same number of negative or positive terms? Do different groups have different ideas about war?

Here is an example of a mind map based on William Shakespeare:

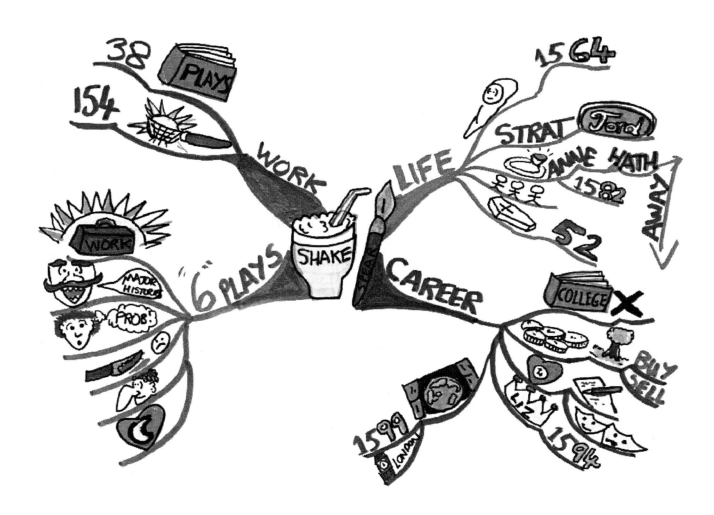

# WAR! WHAT IS IT GOOD FOR?

This is how to make a mind map of your own:

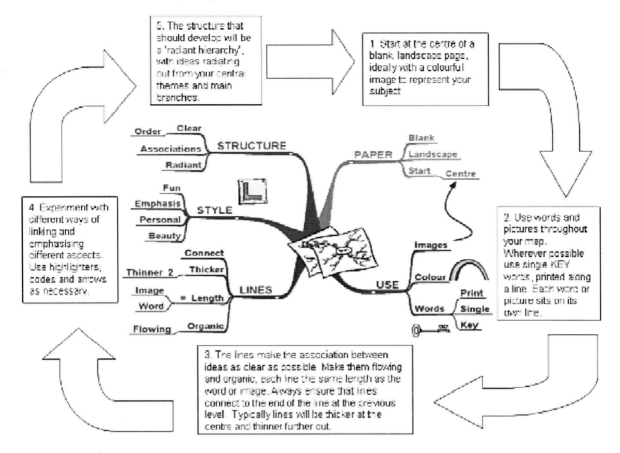

# THINK:

Read the following statements. Tick the box to decide whether you agree or disagree, then discuss your answers as a group. You need to have reasons for your answers. **Are some of the group more in favour of war than others? Why?**

| Statement | Agree | Disagree |
|---|---|---|
| War brings out the best in people. | | |
| War brings out the worst in people. | | |
| War is God's way of punishing people. | | |
| War is a mad game that the world plays. | | |
| It is good that war is horrible. | | |
| An unfair peace is better than a fair war. | | |
| The best way to make sure we have peace is to make sure that we are prepared for war. | | |
| The best way to make sure we have peace is to get rid of all weapons. | | |

# THE CHORUS

Although everything in the play seems to happen really quickly, it actually happened over about six years. To squeeze it all in to one play, Shakespeare uses The Chorus to tell us what is happening and what has happened between scenes.

**The Chorus** is one of the actors who comes on stage at the start of each Act to tell the audience what is going on. This is a very old technique used in plays that dates back to the Ancient Greeks. Shakespeare borrowed (or stole) a lot of their ideas!

**The Chorus** also:
* Sets the scene
* Makes us want to see what happens next
* Tells us what to think about characters and events
* Tries to make us feel as if we are part of the performance
* Makes the play seem more 'epic' like a blockbuster movie

Look at the chorus speeches from the beginning of each Act. Think about how they contain each of the things above. Write down a line from the chorus that shows each one:

| What does the Chorus do? | Where does it do it? | In which act? |
|---|---|---|
| Tells us something that has happened | | |
| Sets the scene | | |
| Makes us want to see what happens next | | |
| Tells us what to think about characters and events | | |
| Tries to make us feel part of the performance | | |
| Makes the play seem more 'epic' | | |

# WILL YOU MARRY ME?

Act 5 scene 2 is very different from the rest of the play. In this scene, Henry persuades Katherine to marry him and a peace agreement is sorted out between France and England. Katherine is reluctant at first and Henry has to try different ways to persuade her.

# TASK 1:

Divide the class into four groups. Each group is to argue a different viewpoint of the scene. The group who 'wins' will be the group who can put across the most convincing argument. **Would the play be better if the scene was left out?**

- **Group 1:**
  Act 5 scene 2 is a let down after the drama of Agincourt. It is a really disappointing way to end the play. Find evidence in the play to support this viewpoint and present it in the debate.

- **Group 2:**
  Henry is behaving out of character in Act 5 scene 2. He made brilliant speeches at Harfleur and Agincourt but here he is muddled in front of a girl. This shows bad writing by Shakespeare. Find evidence in the play to support this viewpoint and present it in the debate.

- **Group 3:**
  Act 5 scene 2 is a charming, funny scene which makes Henry even more human. Find evidence in the play to support this viewpoint and present it in the debate.

- **Group 4:**
  Henry is wrong to force Katherine to marry him when she knows that she is only part of a deal between Henry and her father. Find evidence in the play to support this viewpoint and present it in the debate.

# TASK 2:

Compare Katherine's English lesson in Act 3 scene 4 with the English that she speaks in Act 5 scene 2. Why is it so different?

# TASK 3:

Imagine you are Katherine. Write a letter to a friend in France explaining why you are marrying Henry. Remember: he defeated your father and brother, invaded your country and killed your people. But you're still going to marry him! Why?

# COMEDY IN HENRY V

## WORKSHEET 1

The characters in the play are not all serious. Shakespeare often included groups of 'comic' or 'comedy' characters in his plays in order to relieve the tension between scenes of great drama.

### Characters
Bardolph, Pistol and Nym are basically comic characters. So is Fluellen. Sometimes we see this in the way that they are described, sometimes in what they say.

## TASK:
In groups, look at the following scenes:
Act 2 scene 1; Act 2 scene 3; Act 3 scene 2; Act 4 scene 4; Act 5 scene 1
Each group could look at one particular scene.

**What sort of comedy is being used in your chosen scene?**
e.g. Look for examples of puns, irony, stereotyping, slapstick, farce, mistaken identities and straightforward jokes. Which jokes are easy to find and which had to be explained to you? Why do you think this is?

**How would you make the characters in your chosen scene appear to be funny?**
e.g. Think about how they might be dressed, what their faces might look like etc. Look for clues in the scene that could help you with this. You could draw the character(s) to emphasise the humour in the way they look.

**Choose a section of your scene to act out.**
When you do this, make sure one member of the group is not acting but helping the others to be funny. Present your scene in a way that emphasises facial expressions, the way you stand and move your hands, and voices. You could even use simpler language if you find it easier, but try to keep the point of what Shakespeare has the characters saying.

# COMEDY IN HENRY V

WORKSHEET 2

Examine Henry's joke involving Williams and Fluellen through Act 4 scenes 1, 7 and 8. Note down briefly what happens in each scene. Just look for the parts where Fluellen is involved.

**Act 4 scene 1** (Henry meets Fluellen and he discusses the war with Williams)

**Act 4 scene 7** (Fluellen talks to Henry and Henry sets him up to fight Williams)

**Act 4 scene 8** (Williams and Fluellen nearly fight)

**Remember these points about Fluellen:**

- He starts an argument with MacMorris.
  **Discuss: What is the argument about?**
- He is the victim of Henry's joke with Williams.
  **Discuss: Why does Henry do this?**
- He picks a fight with Pistol about St David's Day.
- He is proud of being Welsh.
  **Discuss: How does Shakespeare show his accent?**
- He thinks he knows everything about war because he has read about it in old books.
  **Discuss: How does Shakespeare show him to be big-headed?**

# COMEDY IN HENRY V

## WORKSHEET 3

Sometimes, Shakespeare creates humour by putting two scenes next to each other to show irony (when someone says something but means something else) or to make a serious point in an amusing way.

**For example, the Chorus at the start of Act 2 says:**

Now all the youth of England are on fire,
And silken dalliance in the wardrobe lies:
Now thrive the armourers, and honour's thought
Reigns solely in the breast of every man.

**However, Act 2 scene 1 then introduces us to Nym, Pistol and Bardolph as cowardly thieves, as we can see when Nym speaks:**

For my part, I care not: I say little; but when time shall serve, there shall be smiles; but that shall be as it may. I dare not fight; but I will wink and hold out mine iron: it is a simple one; but what though? it will toast cheese, and it will endure cold as another man's sword will: and there's an end.

## TASK 1:

Explain the difference between what the Chorus tells the audience to expect and what the audience actually gets when Act 2 scene 1 starts.

## TASK 2:

Compare Henry's speech at the start of Act 3 scene 1 with what Bardolph and Fluellen say straight afterwards. What are the similarities between what the three characters say and what are the differences? **What makes it funny?**

# HENRY: GOOD OR BAD KING?

Some people say that Henry was a good leader. Some people think that Shakespeare's version of Henry is unrealistic or that he is a hypocrite (he doesn't practice what he preaches).

## RESEARCH:
Look up the following words in a good dictionary and write down the definitions.

a.    hypocrite          b.    honour

## DISCUSS:
1.    In what way is Henry a hypocrite?
2.    Is he honourable?

## THINK:
Decide whether the following statements about Henry show him to be a good or bad king. Tick the box that you think is correct.

| Statement | Good | Bad |
|---|---|---|
| He pardons the drunk man who "railed against" him. | | |
| He kills his friends Scroop and Bardolph. | | |
| He lets the people of Harfleur live. | | |
| He talks to his soldiers before they go into battle. | | |
| He leads his men to their deaths. | | |
| He orders that the French prisoners be killed at Agincourt. | | |
| He marries Katherine as part of the French peace agreement. | | |
| When the French King offers him Katherine if he will stop the war, Henry refuses. | | |

Compare Henry to the French King and The Dauphin.
Which statement applies to which character? Tick the box that you think is correct.

| Statement | Henry | French King | Dauphin |
|---|---|---|---|
| He goes to war because he is encouraged by other people. | | | |
| He thinks his enemy is weak and childish. | | | |
| He knows his enemy outnumbers his men but he knows that God is on his side. | | | |
| He goes to war because he wants to prove himself. | | | |
| He is ready to surrender when he thinks that he is defeated. | | | |
| He admires his enemy. | | | |

## DISCUSS:
In what ways are they similar or different to each other? Which character do you think would make the best king? Why?

# HENRY'S TRIAL

**Split the class into two groups.**

Group 1 is the **PROSECUTION** group.
The Prosecution's job is to argue the case FOR Henry, that he is a GOOD leader and king.

# TASK:

Find as much evidence as you can from the play that shows that Henry is a good king. You could write this in your own words but also write down at least three quotations (the exact words that Shakespeare wrote). You will need these later as evidence.

Group 2 is the **DEFENCE** group.
The Defence's job is to argue the case AGAINST Henry, that he is a BAD leader and king.

# TASK:

Find as much evidence as you can from the play that shows that Henry is a bad king. You could write this in your own words but also write down at least three quotations (the exact words that Shakespeare wrote). You will need these later as evidence.

**The Trial:**
From the two sides of the class, select students to take on the roles of judge, jury, defence and prosecution lawyers, and witnesses. Witnesses will be characters from the play – but they can't be anyone who is dead!
**Characters who will say that he is a bad king will be Prosecution witnesses.**
**Characters who will say that he is a good king will be Defence witnesses.**
Each set of witnesses will need to work with students from the Prosecution or Defence group to prepare for the trial.

**Witnesses need to decide:**
What are they going to say?
Lawyers need to decide:
What questions will they ask?

Just like a real trial, set up the class so that each lawyer makes a case, then calls forward witnesses who are then cross-examined. The jury should make notes as the role-play continues, then have some time to make a decision on their verdict. The judge's job is to keep it all under control, and this role could be taken by the Teacher or a very confident member of the class.

# PERFORMING HENRY'S SPEECHES

**Act 3 Scene 1**

"Once more unto the breach..."

**Act 4 Scene 3**

"...we band of brothers"

## TASK:

Divide Henry's speech in either Act 3 scene 1 or Act 4 scene 3 into whole sentences or phrases.

Each member of the class has one sentence or phrase. Memorise it!

You may need a big space for this part. Outside on a sunny day might be a good idea.

- Practice saying the sentence or phrase in as many different ways as possible:

  - Shout it!
  - Whisper it.
  - Say it in a pleading tone.
  - Sing it!
  - Say it in a persuading tone.
  - Say it quickly!
  - Say it slowly.
  - Say it angrily!
  - Say it as if you are apologising.
  - Say it sarcastically.

- Choose a way to say it that you think fits what Henry is saying in that part of the speech.
- Everyone form a circle, standing in the order of the speech. In your circle, decide what you're going to do when you say your line. You could step forward, shake your fist, raise your arms, etc. You decide.
- Go around the circle in order, each person saying his or her sentence in turn.
- You've all performed the speech together!
- Now do the same with the other speech.

# GLOBE RESEARCH SHEET 1
## TEACHER'S VERSION

| QUESTION:<br>Shakespeare's Globe, London | ANSWER: |
|---|---|
| At Shakespeare's Globe in London, how many standing tickets are available for each performance? | 700 |
| Who was the architect for Shakespeare's Globe? | Theo Crosby |
| And the architect for the original Globe? | Peter Street |
| Which play was performed at the original Globe in 1599? | Henry V |
| Write down 3 facts about The Globe | Anything that is factual.<br>www.shakespeares-globe.org/ |
| What is the Supporting Wall? | A wall full of etched signatures of people who have donated to the Globe.<br>www.shakespeares-globe.org/supportus/donations/supportingwall/ |
| When was Henry V performed at the 'new' Globe? | The opening season 1997 |
| Name three areas of the new Globe exhibition. | Costume and clothing, Printing and publishing, Music, Re-building the Globe |
| Who was Edward Alleyn? | Leading actor of the Lord Admirals Men at the Rose Theatre |
| In which other countries are there replicas of the Globe? | Germany and Italy. (USA on the way!)<br>www.en.wikipedia.org/wiki/globe_theatre |

# GLOBE THEATRE: Label Descriptions

## THE GLOBE
## TEACHER'S VERSION

**The Heavens**
The canopy over the stage, decorated with signs of the zodiac. There was a space above here from which actors could be lowered through a trapdoor as gods or angels.

**The Gentlemen's Rooms**
Rich playgoers could sit here on cushions.

**The Trapdoor**
This led down to Hell! It was a room below the stage from where actors playing ghosts, witches and devils could make their entrance.

**The Yard**
A thousand Groundlings would stand here to watch the plays. Noisy and smelly!

**The Musician's Gallery**
Sometimes live music was played here but it was also used for acting as a wall or balcony.

**The Lord's Rooms**
Here was the best place to sit if you were a lord or lady because everyone could see you – but your view might not be very good!

**The Tiring House**
An area behind the stage where costumes and props were kept and actors got changed.

**The Pillars**
There were trunks of oak trees put here to hold up The Heavens. The theatre was meant to be like the universe – divided into Heaven, Earth and Hell.

71

# GLOBE RESEARCH SHEET 2
## TEACHER'S VERSION

| QUESTION:<br>The New Globe, New York | ANSWER: |
|---|---|
| Name 3 of the actors who are supporting the project. | Long list on the home page, left hand side, under 'Friends of the New Globe: artists'<br>www.newglobe.org/ |
| Find the names of 3 other actors from the list that you have heard of and name a film play or TV show that they have been in.<br><br>OR:<br>If you haven't heard of any of them, find out what the 3 actors you have already named have been in. | Hint: Show the students how to type a name into 'Google' or a similar search engine and 'click through' for information. Alternatively, this could be done as a whole class using an interactive whiteboard connected to the internet. A follow-up activity could be to write a short biography of one of the actors. |
| One of the actors who supports the project is Zoe Wanamaker. What is her connection to the Globe in London? | Her father was Sam Wanamaker, who started off the whole rebuilding project in London. |
| **BBC** | |
| What BBC TV comedy features Zoe Wanamaker as the mother of a family? Who does she play in the Harry Potter films? | My Family is the TV show. Hogwarts teacher Madam Hooch is the Harry Potter character. www.bbc.co.uk<br>Click the TV links or type in 'Zoe Wanamaker' into the search box on the home page. |
| In which Doctor Who episode did The Doctor and Martha meet William Shakespeare? | The Shakespeare Code<br>www.bbc.co.uk/doctorwho<br>Click on 'episodes' and follow the links. |
| In that episode, who played William Shakespeare? | Dean Lennox Kelly<br>www.bbc.co.uk/doctorwho/episodes/2007/302.shtml<br>Then click 'Fact File' for the cast list. |
| Write down 3 interesting facts about this episode of Doctor Who. | Anything from the 'Did You Know?' section of the 'Fact File' as above.<br>The episode is available on DVD.<br>Follow-up work could involve view and review of the episode. |

5

# HENRY V - THE STORY
## TEACHER'S VERSION

Answers to the questions are below.

**1. Name all four of Henry's friends from when he was younger.**
Pistol, Bardolph, Nym and Falstaff.

**2. Which friend does he have executed and what was his crime?**
Bardolph – for stealing money (or a 'pax'- a cross) from a church.

**3. Which friend dies before they go to France?**
Falstaf – of a broken heart due to being rejected by Henry.

**4. How does Henry manage to defeat the town of Harfleur?**
He gives a rousing speech to his men, which spurs them on.

**5. What does Henry do on the evening before the Battle of Agincourt?**
He visits his soldiers in disguise and argues about his responsibilities to them in war.

**6. Who are killed by the French in battle?**
The Earl of Suffolk and the Duke of York.
They also kill the boys, who are used as heralds and messengers.

**7. Why does Henry have all the French prisoners killed?**
The French killed the defenceless boys, who are used as heralds and messengers. This is against the rules of war.

**8. How many French soldiers are killed in battle?**
Ten thousand.

**9. Who does Henry ask to marry him at the end of the play?**
Princess Katherine.

**10. Which countries will Henry VI rule?**
England and France.

# FAMILY TREE
## TEACHER'S VERSION

Answers to the questions are below.

**1. What are the titles of Henry V's two brothers?**

Henry's two brothers are: The Duke of Gloucester
and The Duke of Bedford

**2. How is the Duke of Exeter related to Henry V?**

The Duke of Exeter is Henry's uncle.

**3. What is the name of Henry V's wife?**

Henry's wife is Katherine of France.

**4. After Henry V gets married, who is his brother-in-law?**

His brother-in-law is Charles VII (The Dauphin).

**5. Which two women in the family tree have similar names?**

Queen Isabella and Queen Isabel have similar names.

**6. Explain in what way they are related to Henry V.**

Queen Isabella is Henry's Great-Great-Grandmother. Queen Isabel is Henry's Mother-in-Law

**7. Which of Henry's relatives are not in the play?**

The relatives who are not in the play are: Edward II; Queen Isabella; Edward III; John of Gaunt Duke of
Lancaster; Edmund Duke of York; (Edward Duke of York does appear in the play); Henry IV.

# THE BATTLE OF AGINCOURT
## WORKSHEET - TEACHER'S VERSION

**The Salic Law (In brief)**

A tradition in some royal families of Europe, which prohibited females and descendants in the female line from inheriting land, titles, and offices.

France and Spain, especially in the houses of Valois and Bourbon, followed the Salic Law. A claim of Edward III to the French throne through the descent of his mother, Isabella, was rejected in France because of the Salic Law, and the dispute led to the Hundred Years' War.

When Isabella II of Spain succeeded to the throne, after the Salic Law was rescinded, the Carlists rebelled.

When Victoria became Queen of England, she was not also ruler of Hanover, as her ancestors back to George I had been, because Hanover followed the Salic Law.

The actual Salic Law, a pre-Roman Germanic code from the Salian Franks and instituted under Clovis, dealt with property inheritance, but not the passing of titles.

More details about Salic Law can be found here:
www.heraldica.org/topics/france/salic.htm

**The Hundred Years' War**

Answers to the questions are **in bold** below.

How long was the Hundred Years' War?
**The Hundred Years' War lasted 116 years until 1453.**

When did it start, and who started it?
**The Hundred Years' War was started by Philip VI of France in 1337.**

Where was the last stronghold of the English in France?
**Calais.**

When was it surrendered?
**1558.**

Which famous Frenchwoman led the French armies to victory at Orleans?
**Joan of Arc.**

More details about the Hundred Years' War can be found here:
**http://ehistory.osu.edu/middleages/hundredyearswar/overview.cfm**

# THE LONGBOW
## TEACHER'S VERSION

| Date | Timeline of the Longbow |
|---|---|
| 50,000BC | Arrowheads found in Tunisia, Algeria and Morocco |
| Circa 3,000BC | Longbow first appears in Europe |
| Circa 2,690BC | Evidence of longbow being used in Somerset, England |
| 950AD | Historical evidence of crossbows in France |
| 1066 | Battle of Hastings |
| 1100's | Henry I introduces law that meant any archer was freed if he killed another archer whilst practising |
| Circa 1300 | Edward I bans all sports other than archery on Sundays |
| 1340 | Start of The One Hundred Years War |
| 1346 | Crécy |
| 1356 | Poitiers |
| 1363 | All Englishmen ordered to practice archery on Sunday and holidays |
| 1377 | First mention of Robyn Hode in the poem Piers Plowman written by William Langland |
| 1414 | Agincourt |
| 1453 | English archers killed by cannon and lances attacking French artillery position at Castillon, the last battle of The One Hundred Years War |
| 1472 | English ships ordered to import wood needed to make bows |
| 1508 | To increase use of longbows, crossbows are banned in England |
| 1644 | Tippermuir - Last battle involving the longbow |
| 17th Century | Muskets become more popular |

# ANSWERS:

Answers to the questions are **in bold** below.

1.  How long was an average Longbow?

    **6ft**

2.  Name three woods that a longbow can be made from.

    **Yew, Ash, Elm, Wych Elm, Oak, Ask and Maple.**

3.  How many pieces of wood are used in a 'self-bow'?

    **One**

4.  Name three major battles between England and France where the longbow was used.

    **Crecy, Poitiers and Agincourt.**

5.  What woods were arrows usually made from?

    **Usually Ash, Oak or Birch.**

6.  What was the maximum range of a longbow?

    **400 metres. From 200 metres a longbow could penetrate over one inch of solid oak!!**

# HENRY: FOLLOW THE LEADER
## WORKSHEET 3 - TEACHER'S VERSION

Look again at the list. In the play, Henry shows some of these qualities, but sometimes he doesn't. How many of these 'rules' does he break? Answers are below.

| The qualities that Henry should have. | Does Henry show these qualities? Tick yes or no. | | Write your reasons in this column. Explain what Henry does or says. |
| --- | --- | --- | --- |
| | Yes | No | |
| The King must show that he is Christian and support the Christian Church. | Yes | | He agrees to the Archbishop's and Bishop's wishes in Act 1 scene 2. |
| The King must know a lot about theology (religion). | Hmm | Maybe! | Although he persuades his men to fight in God's name and sees himself as representing God, he does not show that he studies religion closely. |
| The King must show mercy and never take personal revenge. | Hmm | Maybe! | Henry sets free a prisoner on the advice of the traitors (Act 2 scene 2) and allows the French to go onto the battlefield to count up their dead when they are defeated (Act 4 scene 7) – BUT he also angrily sentences the traitors to death and has Bardolph hanged for stealing. |
| The King must be very self-controlled and not lose his temper. | Hmm | Maybe! | Most of the time this is a 'yes' but he allows the Dauphin's insult to make him angry and he decides to invade France partly because of this (Act 1 scene 2). |
| He should take counsel (advice) from wise men. | Yes | | He takes advice from the Archbishop and Bishop, as well as his Dukes – especially his uncle the Duke of Exeter. |
| He should be friendly with the common people but not let it affect his job as King. | Yes | | We see this very clearly in Act 4 scene 1 when he goes among his men in disguise. BUT he rejected his old friends Falstaff, Bardolph, Pistol and Nym when he became King. |
| He must seek to defend and protect the state (his country). | Hmm | Maybe! | Is the war about protecting England or about attacking France? |
| He should get rid of bad influences around him – e.g. people who are unhelpful or flatter (suck up to) him too much. | Yes | | He ended his friendship with Falstaff, Bardolph, Nym and Pistol, all men who either drank a lot or were thieves. |
| He should be concerned about how war will affect his people and his country. | Yes | | This is why he goes to see his men in disguise before the battle of Agincourt, although he disagrees with them about how responsible he is if they die. |
| He should be married. | Yes | | He isn't married when the play begins, but he soon puts that right by the end of the play. |

# ENGLISH ROYAL CHARACTERS: DUKES AND EARLS
## TEACHER'S VERSION

Answers to the tasks are below.

## TASKS:

| Look at Act 2 scene 2. What does Exeter do in this scene? |
| --- |

He arrests the three traitors on Henry's behalf.

Teaching hint: Show the class this scene from the Kenneth Branagh film version of Henry V. Brian Blessed's performance shows disgust and anger in just a few lines. He tears away their chains of office and slaps one of them.

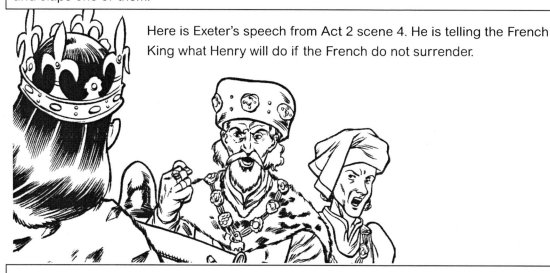

Here is Exeter's speech from Act 2 scene 4. He is telling the French King what Henry will do if the French do not surrender.

| Underline the words that are about suffering, violence and pain. |
| --- |

<u>Bloody constraint</u>; for if you **hide the crown**
**Even in your hearts**, there will he **rake for it**:
Therefore **in <u>fierce tempest</u> is he coming**,
In thunder and in earthquake, like a Jove,
That, if requiring fail, he will compel;
And bids you, in **the bowels of the Lord**,
Deliver up the crown, and to take mercy
On the <u>poor souls</u> for whom this **hungry <u>war</u>**
Opens **his vasty jaws**; and **on your head**
**Turning** the <u>widows' tears</u>, the <u>orphans' cries</u>
The <u>dead men's blood</u>, the <u>pining maidens groans</u>,
For husbands, fathers and betrothed lovers,
That **shall be swallow'd in this controversy**.
This is his claim, his <u>threatening</u> and my message;

**Write down a simile from the speech:**
"like a Jove" (like a god controlling the wind and storms)

**Write down three metaphors from the speech:**
See left. Metaphors are in bold.

**Teaching hint:**
Discuss the examples listed here. Ask students to try to explain what two things are being compared in each metaphor, and what each one tells us about Henry.

| Describe in your own words what Exeter is threatening that Henry will do: |
| --- |

An ideal answer here will describe how Exeter is using metaphor to make Henry seem like a vengeful god exacting his justice on the French, giving the impression that Henry will attack them on his own with such power that it will be as if he is eating the French men, leaving their women and children to cry alone.

# THE ARCHBISHOP OF CANTERBURY
# AND THE BISHOP OF ELY
## TEACHER'S VERSION

## ANSWERS:

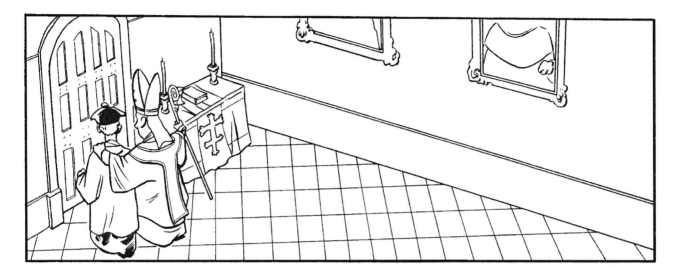

1. **Who was Alexander the Great and what did he do to become famous?**
   He was one of the most successful military commanders in history, and was undefeated in battle. By the time of his death, he had conquered most of the world known to the ancient Greeks.

2. **What was the Gordian Knot and what did it have to do with Alexander?**
   The Gordian Knot is a metaphor for an intractable problem, solved by a bold stroke ("cutting the Gordian knot"). Alexander untied (or cut) the knot, becoming King of Asia as prophesied.

3. **What does Canterbury mean when he mentions the Gordian Knot in his description of Henry?**
   That he could 'untie' any complicated problem.

4. **What does Ely mean when he compares Henry to a strawberry growing "underneath the nettle"?**
   That by surrounding himself with unsuitable companions, Henry's goodness and intelligence was hidden by their ignorance and bad behaviour, but was growing all of that time.

# PISTOL, NYM AND BARDOLPH
## TEACHER'S VERSION

## ANSWERS:

### Act 2 scene 1
1.    His sword. He is ready to fight.
2.    Pistol married Hostess Quickly, to whom Nym was engaged.
3.    Accept almost anything between 'Enter Pistol' and 'Enter Boy'.

### Act 2 scene 3
4.    Falstaff has died of a broken heart after the King's rejection of him.
5.    She felt under the covers of the bed and he was as cold as stone, and he cried out against women and wine ("sack").
6.    They talk about his humour, his drinking, his women, his loyalty to the king and sadness at being rejected.

### Act 3 scene 2
7.    Bardolph is a coward and red-faced who provokes but does not fight. Pistol has a big mouth but does not follow up with action. Nym does not say his prayers so that he isn't called a coward. Nym and Bardolph are both thieves, and the Boy is afraid that he will be dragged along with them.
8.    It should be a 'yes' really, because he is sensible enough to see that staying in their company will lead to trouble.

### Act 3 scene 6
9.    Bad luck has caught up with him and he has been arrested and will be executed for theft.
10.   He is asking Fluellen to speak up for Bardolph to prevent his death.
11.   Fluellen refuses, "for discipline ought to be used".

### Act 4 scenes 1 and 4
12.   "Tell him I'll knock his leek about his pate (his head) upon Saint Davy's Day".
13.   He takes a French soldier prisoner. Jokes come from the language barrier and misunderstanding of words – e.g. "Fer", "firk", "ferret".

# THE FRENCH COURT
## TEACHER'S VERSION

## ANSWERS:

### Act 2 scene 4

1.    The Dauphin; tennis balls
2.    The Constable
3.    French King
4.    "…she is so idly king'd,
      Her sceptre so fantastically borne,
      By a vain, giddy, shallow humorous youth,
      That fear attends her not".
5.    The Dukes of Berri, Bretagne, Brabant and Orleans, and The Dauphin

### Katherine

Katherine does not appear until Act 3 scene 4, where she is being taught English quite badly by Alice.

1.    Mostly body parts – e.g. 'hand', 'elbow' and 'chin'

2.    Again, mostly body parts – e.g. neck – "nick"; elbow – "D'elbow"; chin – "sin"

3.    She can construct sentences. Any answer that draws attention to particular things that she is able to communicate in English or words that she says differently in Act 5 compared to Act 2 would be good.

4.    Here are three sentences that Katherine says. Rewrite them in standard English:
      **Answers in bold**.

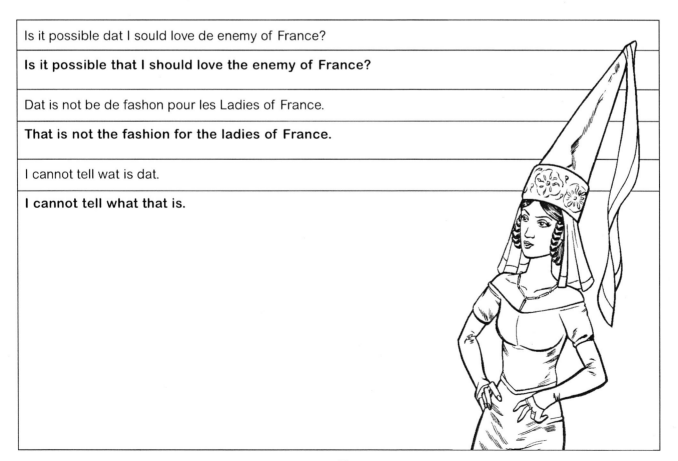

| |
|---|
| Is it possible dat I sould love de enemy of France? |
| **Is it possible that I should love the enemy of France?** |
| Dat is not be de fashon pour les Ladies of France. |
| **That is not the fashion for the ladies of France.** |
| I cannot tell wat is dat. |
| **I cannot tell what that is.** |

# SHAKESPEARE'S LANGUAGE
## TEACHER'S VERSION

Shakespeare wrote his plays differently from the way plays are written today. Many of the lines spoken by characters are in a form of poetry called **blank verse**. Shakespeare wrote Henry V using a mixture of blank verse and prose. The parts of the play that look like poetry are in blank verse.

Shakespeare's version of blank verse usually has ten syllables in each line. Each syllable is like a beat of a drum. Try reading the following lines aloud whilst tapping out the beat with your hand:

| 1 | 2 | 3 | 4 | 5 | 6 | 7 | 8 | 9 | 10 |
|---|---|---|---|---|---|---|---|---|---|
| Once | more | un | to | the | breach | dear | friends, | once | more |
| Or | close | up | the | wall | with | our | Eng | lish | dead. |

Each pair of syllables is called an **iamb**. In each pair, one syllable is stressed and the other is unstressed. Try reading the above lines aloud to see which syllables are stressed. The style of having blank verse with ten syllables per line is called **iambic pentameter**. This gives the words a rhythm that is a bit musical but also sounds like natural speech. The rhythm made it easier for actors to remember and to say aloud, especially as they had to perform in the open air and they didn't have microphones!

**Teacher's Note:**

An iamb is also often called an iambic foot. A good way to demonstrate the stresses to pupils is to imagine a footstep: the heel (stressed syllable) touches the ground first; the sole (unstressed syllable) follows, then it's on to the next step. An active way to experience this is to have the class walk around a large space, reciting the lines in time with their steps. Exaggerate the stresses when saying them aloud. If every syllable is unstressed, the reading sounds mumbled. If every syllable is stressed, it sounds loud and robotic.

# TASKS:

**Teacher's Notes**

1. Encourage the pupils to experiment with different readings. Demonstrate how different readings can suggest different meanings. For example(stressed syllables in **bold**):
   **Once** more **un**to the **breach** emphasises the 'once', suggesting it is the last push;
   Whereas: Once **more** unto the **breach** emphasises 'more', suggesting that Henry will keep on going and won't give up.

2. For 'acting out' their speeches or dialogue, pupils will need lots of space so that they can be as declamatory (i.e. loud) as possible.

3. The characters who speak in blank verse tend to be important characters such as royalty and for important scenes or speeches. Big speeches and soliloquies will always be in blank verse. Shakespeare used prose usually for comic characters (in this case Bardolph, Nym, Pistol etc) or for characters of lower social status. Blank verse is generally used to show social status or to elevate the language to sound more important or dramatic. It doesn't lend itself as well to comedy as prose does.

4. Henry speaks prose when he meets Pistol and the other soldiers in Act 4 scene 1. He is pretending to be one of the common men here, so he changes his language appropriately.

# HENRY V SPELLING JUMBLE - ANAGRAMS
## TEACHER'S VERSION

| Jumbled Spelling | Correct Spelling |
|---|---|
| FORE GODS CUTE LUKE | DUKE OF GLOUCESTER |
| F: THY HITHER FEN | HENRY THE FIFTH |
| FISH POLE BOY | BISHOP OF ELY |
| U HAD PIN | DAUPHIN |
| FEAR HURL | HARFLEUR |
| CROOL DROPS | LORD SCROOP |
| CUGO TRAIN | AGINCOURT |
| DR. B.P. HALO | BARDOPLPH |
| CRY! RACE FOR POSH, THIN BUBA! | ARCHBISHOP OF CANTERBURY |
| I HATE RENK | KATHERINE |
| BARF! I GORED CAMEL! | EARL OF CAMBRIDGE |

FISH POLE BOY

# MISSING WORDS
## TEACHER'S VERSION

To complete the sentences below, underline the correct word in the box, then write it in the gap. Be careful – there are some traps in the box!

**The answers are in bold.**

1.  'Dauphin' is the French word for **prince**.

2.  "Once more unto the **breach**".

3.  "But when the blast of war blows in our ears,
    Then imitate the **action** of the **tiger**".

4.  "The strawberry grows underneath the **nettle**,
    And wholesome berries thrive and **ripen** best,
    Neighbour'd by fruit of baser **quality**".

5.  The Duke of Exeter is Henry's **uncle**.

6.  Henry marries Princess **Katherine**.

7.  The French King thinks that King Henry is **strong** and "bred out of that **bloody** strain", meaning that Henry could be as powerful as his ancestor, **Edward** Black Prince of **Wales**.

8.  Henry threatens the governor of **Harfleur** that he will see old men "taken by their silver **beards** and their most reverend **heads** dash'd to the walls".

9.  Henry gets Fluellen to wear Williams' **glove** in his **cap**.

10. The Battle of **Agincourt** was fought on Saint **Crispin**'s Day.

# WHAT HAPPENS NEXT?
## TASK 1 - TEACHER'S VERSION

**Teacher's Note**

This is an activity that is primarily a reading activity disguised as art. The range of scenes covered by the cards home in on some of the key moments, encouraging the pupils to make connections between different parts of the text. A knowledge of the text will be needed to be able to complete the first task 'What Happens Next?'

Suggested answers are below.

| Comic Card | **WHAT IS HAPPENING?** Describe in your own words. Try to explain what is going on in each panel and what characters are saying. Can you remember what happens next? |
|---|---|
| **CARD 1** | In **Act 1 scene 2**, an Ambassador from France comes to see Henry. He presents him with a present from the Dauphin: a chest that contains tennis balls. This is in fact an insult to Henry, suggesting that he would be better off playing games rather than trying to be a king. This shows how young Henry is and how much he is underestimated by his enemies. Henry politely thanks the Ambassador. **What happens next?** Henry makes a big speech where he threatens to turn the balls into bullets and make the France pay for this insult with violence. |
| **CARD 2** | In **Act 3 scene 3**, Henry is at the gates of the walled town of Harfleur. On this page, he is making a dramatic speech where he threatens to allow his soldiers to attack young women and kill old men and children (Also see the Henry's Speeches section). The Governor of the town surrenders and the Henry tells him to open the gates to the town. **What happens next?** This is the end of the scene. Henry orders Exeter to stay in the town and guard it against the French. The next scene relieves the tension by introducing us to Katherine as she learns English – badly. |
| **CARD 3** | In **Act 4 scene 1**, Henry has borrowed a cloak and has gone into the soldiers' camp in disguise so that he can find out how the men are feeling about the battle that they are about to face. He is challenged by Pistol, who asks him who he is. He lies and says his name is Harry Le Roy. On this page, Pistol talks about how much he admires the King and he threatens to fight Fluellen. **What happens next?** Henry overhears Gower and Fluellen talking and admires Fluellen's attitude to the enemy. He then meets Williams and Bates and gets involved in an argument with them about whether it is the King's fault if they die (Also see Henry's Debate section). |
| **CARD 4** | In **Act 5 scene 2**, Henry is in the middle of persuading Katherine to marry him. He tries a number of tactics. Here, he is trying to show her that he is a normal man underneath the crown and flatters her. This works and she kisses him. **What happens next?** Burgundy warns Henry to take things slowly with Katherine, but the French King agrees to allow the couple to get married. |

# WHAT HAPPENS NEXT?
## TASK 2 - TEACHER'S VERSION

**Teacher's Notes**

Task 2 extends the activity further for stronger readers. There are a number of ways in which pupils can access this activity. Different ability groups could be given different versions of the task to do:

a.      **Version 1** – Direct pupils towards the relevant pages in the original text of the play. Pupils then copy a key sentence from each piece of dialogue onto a blank word balloon, and stick it on to the sheet next to the character who is speaking. You might prefer to enlarge the artwork to A3 to make this easier. This involves a level of selection rather than simply copying out.

b.      **Version 2** – More able readers could identify the relevant passages as above, but translate the text into modern English before writing it into the word balloons.

c.      **Version 3** – For a bit more fun, the text could be translated into their own more informal language. This could be more 'street', but beware! This would need clear teacher guidance and / or intervention to avoid potentially inappropriate language.

The word balloons provided are suggested shapes. Pupils could draw their own in varying shapes and cut them out in order the fit the page better.

**The Comic Script:**

Part of the original comic script for this section of the play is on page 83. Included here are the different versions of the dialogue which you could use in part or in whole to help guide the pupils.

# FOLLOW-UP TASK:

- Choose another scene, or part of a scene, from the play.
- Think about what characters are doing in this part of the scene and what they are saying. Are they angry? Are they happy? Are they walking? What is in the background?
- Design a comic page showing what is happening in this part of the scene. Decide what you are going to write in each word balloon. Aim to have one or two word balloons in each picture.
- You could use Shakespeare's original language or write what the characters say in your own words.
- Either draw your own boxes for the pictures or use the sample grid.

# COMIC PAGE GRID

# COMIC SCRIPT - FROM ACT 5 SCENE 2

**515.** Katharine tries to pull away from Henry. This time he's amused by her erratic coquettish behaviour and he rises and holds onto her.

| | | |
|---|---|---|
| KATHARINE | No, My Lord! You should not lower yourself by kissing the hand of one of your humble servants. | *Stop, my lord, stop, stop! My goodness, I would not 'ave you lower yourself by kissing 'and de one of Your Majesty's 'umble servants. Excusez-moi, I beg you, mon powerful lord.* | *Laissez, mon seigneur, laissez, laissez! Ma foi, je ne veux point que vous abaissez votre grandeur en baisant la main d'une de votre seigneurie indigne serviteur. Excusez-moi, je vous supplie, mon très-puissant seigneur.* |
| HENRY | Then I'll kiss your lips. | Then I'll kiss your lips, Kate. | Then I will kiss your lips, Kate. |

**516.** Close on them. Katharine turns her head away from his lips. Henry keeps his eyes on Katharine, though he talks to Alice, who's watching in bg.

| | QUICK TEXT | PLAIN ENGLISH TEXT | ORIGINAL TEXT |
|---|---|---|---|
| KATHARINE | We cannot kiss before marriage | *For ladies et gentilmen to kiss before le marriage is not le raison de France.* | *Les dames et demoiselles pour être baisées devant leur noces, il n'est pas la coutume de France.* |
| HENRY | Is this true? | Dear lady, interpreter, what's she saying? | Madame my interpreter, what says she? |
| ALICE | It is not be the fashion for ladies of France...to, how you say... | *Dat it is not be de fashion pour les ladies of France... I cannot tell vat is "baiser" en English...* | *Dat it is not be de fashion pour les ladies in France,— I cannot tell vat is baiser en Anglish.* |

**517.** Henry continues to hold onto Katharine, his arm round her waist, while talking to Alice.

| | | | |
|---|---|---|---|
| HENRY | To kiss | To kiss | To kiss. |
| ALICE | Your Majesty understands better than me. | Your Majesty understands better than me. | *Your Majestee entendre bettre que moi.* |
| HENRY | It's not fashionable for the girls of France to kiss before they're married. Is that what she says? | It's not fashionable for the girls of France to kiss before they are married, would she say? | It is not a fashion for the maids in France to kiss before they are married, would she say? |
| ALICE | *Oui, indeed!* | *Oui, vraiment.* | *Oui, vraiment.* |

**518.** Henry releases Katharine's waist, but holds onto her hands. They hold hands at arms length, looking directly at each other.

| | | | |
|---|---|---|---|
| HENRY | **Oh Kate!** Kings take no notice of customs. You and I don't need to worry about such things. No one will dare complain about what we do. So, kiss me! | **Oh Kate!** Listen, narrow-minded customs give in to great kings. Dear Kate, you and I shouldn't be confined by what's "fashionable". We **make** 'fashion', Kate. Who we are will silence anyone who even thinks about complaining, and now I'll silence you for taking the side of your country's "fashion" and denying me a kiss. Slowly and willingly... kiss me. | O Kate, nice customs curtsy to great kings. Dear Kate, you and I cannot be confined within the weak list of a country's fashion. We are the makers of manners, Kate; and the liberty that follows our places stops the mouth of all find-faults, as I will do yours, for upholding the nice fashion of your country in denying me a kiss; therefore, patiently, and yielding. |

**519.** Close on Henry and Katharine as they kiss. This time she doesn't resist.

**520.** Henry stands back and looks at her, still holding her hands.

| | QUICK TEXT | PLAIN ENGLISH TEXT | ORIGINAL TEXT |
|---|---|---|---|
| HENRY | There's witchcraft in your lips, Kate. They say there's more eloquence in the sweet touch of them, than in all the speeches of the French council. They could influence me more than a carriage-full of kings. | You have witchcraft in your lips, Kate. There's more eloquence in the sweet touch of them, than in all the speeches of the French council. They'd influence me more quicker than a whole delegation of kings. | You have witchcraft in your lips, Kate: there is more eloquence in the sugar touch of them than in the tongues of the French council; and they should sooner persuade Harry of England than a general petition of monarchs. |

# HENRY V QUIZ
## TEACHER'S VERSION

| No. | Question | Answer |
|-----|----------|--------|
| 1 | Which device did Shakespeare use to introduce each Act? | b. a chorus |
| 2 | Canterbury claims that Henry can claim the French throne because of a law that stopped a family's inheritance from being passed on to: | c. women |
| 3 | What is this law called? | a. The Salic Law |
| 4 | Which three characters plot to kill Henry? | c. Earl of Cambridge, Sir Thomas Gray and Lord Scroop |
| 5 | Who does Henry have executed for stealing from a church? | c. Bardolph |
| 6 | On which day does the Battle of Agincourt take place? | c. St Crispin's Day |
| 7 | Who does Henry say "come pouring like the tide into a breach" every time the English go to war? | a. The Scottish |
| 8 | Which of these characters used to be Henry's friends? | c. Bardolph, Pistol and Falstaff |
| 9 | Which of Henry's old friends died in his bed, heartbroken that Henry rejected him? | c. Falstaff |
| 10 | Do most characters describe Henry as: | a. a perfect Christian ruler |
| 11 | To which characters does Henry say the following? "I will weep for thee; For this revolt of thine, methinks, is like Another fall of man." | b. the three traitors |
| 12 | What does Bates mean when he says "if his cause be wrong, our obedience to the King wipes the crime of it out of us"? | a. We won't be to blame because we're just following orders. |

# THE CHORUS
## TEACHER'S VERSION

**Teacher's Note**

Below are examples of possible answers that could be used and discussed with the class. In the second column, ideally students need to locate a sentence (which may cover more than one line) to use as a quotation.

| What does the Chorus do? | Where does it do it? | In which act? |
|---|---|---|
| Tells us something that has happened | "…thy fault France hath in thee found out, A nest of hollow bosoms…" (Henry discovers that France has paid 3 of his men to betray him and get him killed) | Act 2 |
| Sets the scene | "Suppose, that you have seen The well-appointed King at Hampton pier, Embark his royalty: and his brave fleet… …Hear the shrill whistle… …behold the threaden sails" | Act 3 |
| Makes us want to see what happens next | "Behold… A little touch of Harry in the night. And so our scene must to the battle fly…" (Hints at Harry's visit to the camp in disguise, suggesting some secret mystery) | Act 4 |
| Tells us what to think about characters and events | "…treacherous crowns, and three corrupted men…" (negative impressions of the 3 traitors created by the adjectives "treacherous" and "corrupted") | Act 2 |
| Tries to make us feel part of the performance | "For 'tis your thoughts that now must deck our Kings, Carry them here and there: jumping o'er times; Turning th' accomplishment of many years Into an hour-glass…" (asking the audience to forgive the limitations of the actors and to use their imaginations) | Act 1 (Prologue) |
| Makes the play seem more 'epic' | "O for a Muse of Fire, that would ascend The brightest Heaven of invention…" (strong imagery – metaphor etc) | Act 1 (Prologue) |

# FOLLOW-UP:

**Put the class into five groups.** Each group takes one of the Chorus speeches, highlighting or underlining examples of each of the above in the speech. These could be colour-coded so that one person in each group could take one aspect of what the Chorus is doing in a reading of the speech.

**Each group presents a reading** of their speech, each student reading their relevant lines (these could be edited versions of the speeches).

**Present the speeches in order.** Discuss whether they tell the complete story or not.

# COMEDY IN HENRY V
## WORKSHEET 3 - TEACHER'S VERSION

Sometimes, Shakespeare creates humour by putting two scenes next to each other to show irony (when someone says something but means something else) or to make a serious point in an amusing way.

**For example, the Chorus at the start of Act 2 says:**

Now all the youth of England are on fire,
And silken dalliance in the wardrobe lies:
Now thrive the armourers, and honour's thought
Reigns solely in the breast of every man.

**However, Act 2 scene 1 then introduces us to Nym, Pistol and Bardolph as cowardly thieves, as we can see when Nym speaks:**

For my part, I care not: I say little; but when
time shall serve, there shall be smiles; but that
shall be as it may. I dare not fight; but I will
wink and hold out mine iron: it is a simple one; but
what though? it will toast cheese, and it will
endure cold as another man's sword will: and
there's an end.

# TASK 1:
Explain the difference between what the Chorus tells the audience to expect and what the audience actually gets when Act 2 scene 1 starts.

# TASK 2:
Compare Henry's speech at the start of Act 3 scene 1 with what Bardolph and Fluellen say straight afterwards. What are the similarities between what the three characters say and what are the differences? **What makes it funny?**

---

**Teacher's Note**
ACT 3 SCENE 1: Note that Bardolph and Fluellen echo Henry's words with much more economy, but each has interpreted the speech differently. Bardolph repeats the instruction to fight on, and Fluellen understands it as disciplining lazy men, whereas it is meant to inspire them.

**HENRY:**     Once more unto the breach, dear friends, once more;
                    Or close the wall up with our English dead.

**BARDOLPH:**  On, on, on, on, on! to the breach, to the breach!

**FLUELLEN:**   Up to the breach, you dogs! avaunt, you cullions!

---

# HENRY: GOOD OR BAD KING?
## TEACHER'S VERSION

## RESEARCH:

Look up the following words in a good dictionary and write down the definitions.

a.    hypocrite          b.    honour

**Teacher's Note**

If you are using an interactive whiteboard with internet access, use www.dictionary.com to discuss the definitions as a group and relate the following discussion to these central definitions.

## THINK:

Decide whether the following statements about Henry show him to be a good or bad king. Tick the box that you think is correct.

**Teacher's Note**

The 'correct' answers are marked with an 'x' below. Where there is more than one 'X', the answer can be debated. For example, Scroop and Bardolph committed a crime. Should Henry treat his friends differently from other criminals? Does he really love Katherine?

| Statement | Good | Bad |
| --- | --- | --- |
| He pardons the drunk man who "railed against" him. | x | |
| He kills his friends Scroop and Bardolph. | x | x |
| He lets the people of Harfleur live. | x | |
| He talks to his soldiers before they go into battle. | x | |
| He leads his men to their deaths. | | x |
| He orders that the French prisoners be killed at Agincourt. | | x |
| He marries Katherine as part of the French peace agreement. | x | x |
| When the French King offers him Katherine if he will stop the war, Henry refuses. | x | |

Compare Henry to the French King and The Dauphin.
The correct answers are marked with an 'X' below.

| Statement | Henry | French King | Dauphin |
| --- | --- | --- | --- |
| He goes to war because he is encouraged by other people. | x | x | |
| He thinks his enemy is weak and childish. | | x | |
| He knows his enemy outnumbers his men but he knows that God is on his side. | x | | |
| He goes to war because he wants to prove himself. | x | | x |
| He is ready to surrender when he thinks that he is defeated. | x | x | |
| He admires his enemy. | | x | |

## DISCUSS:

In what ways are they similar or different to each other? Which character do you think would make the best king? Why?

**Teacher's Note**

Encourage students to come up with their own conclusions – e.g. the French King retains his dignity and surrenders to avoid further bloodshed, so is he a better King?

# COLOURING PAGE 1

# COLOURING PAGE 2

# COLOURING PAGE 3

# EDUCATIONAL LINKS

## PROMOTING LITERACY IN THE CLASSROOM:-

### Graphic Novels for Multiple Literacies

www.readingonline.org/newliteracies/jaal/11-02_column/

In an increasingly visual culture, literacy educators can profit from the use of graphic novels in the classroom, especially for young adults. Educators need not worry that graphic novels discourage text reading. Lavin (1998) even suggested that reading graphic novels might require more complex cognitive skills than the reading of text alone.                    **Gretchen E. Schwarz**

### Classics as graphic novels? Have your say!

www.nate.org.uk/site/index.php?NewsID=000110

A national voice on key issues affecting English teaching. NATE is also an active member of the International Federation of the Teachers of English where it seeks to share the experience of English teachers in the UK and learn from teachers in diverse parts of the world.     **NATE News**

### Graphic novels - engaging readers and encouraging literacy

www.ltscotland.org.uk/literacy/findresources/graphicnovels/index.asp

The showcase resource highlights how graphic novels can be used throughout the curriculum.
                    **Learning and Teaching Scotland**

### Graphic Novels across the curriculum

www.ltscotland.org.uk/literacy/images/Graphic%20novels%20across%20the%20curriculum_tcm4-402928.doc
                    **Mel Gibson**

### Expanding Literacies through Graphic Novels

www.ncte.org/Library/files/Free/recruitment/EJ0956Expanding.pdf

Gretchen Schwarz offers a rationale, based on the need for current students to learn multiple literacies, for the use of graphic novels in the high school English class. She highlights several titles, suggests possible classroom strategies, and discusses some of the obstacles teachers may face in adding graphic novels to their curriculum.                    **Gretchen E. Schwarz**

### Eek! Comics in the Classroom!

www.education-world.com/a_curr/profdev/profdev105.shtml

More and more teachers are finding that once-maligned comics, and their big brothers graphic novels, can be effective tools for teaching a multitude of literacy skills to students with a variety of learning needs.                    **Education World**

### Using Comics and Graphic Novels in the Classroom

www.ncte.org/pubs/chron/highlights/122031.htm

Educators also see the educational potential of comics and graphic novels. They can help with building complex reading skills, according to Shelley Hong Xu, associate professor in the department of teacher education at California State University, Long Beach. She says that graphic novels and comics should have a classroom role similar to other children's literature.
                    **The National Council of Teachers of English (NCTE)**

### Getting graphic! Using graphic novels to promote literacy with pre teens and teens

http://findarticles.com/p/articles/mi_m0PBX/is_4_38/ai_n6123048

Getting Graphic! also tackles the big question: are graphic novels, aka comic books, "junk literature for children," or do they have a "cultural and educational value and belong on the shelves of libraries across the nation"?                    **Michele Gorman**

## Comics in Education
www.humblecomics.com/comicsedu/
> The potency of the picture story is not a matter of modern theory but of anciently established truth. Before man thought in words, he felt in pictures..          **Gene Yang**

## Going Graphic - Comics at Work in the Multilingual Classroom
http://college.heinemann.com/shared/onlineresources/E00475/chapter2.pdf
> Theory, research, practice, guidelines and resources for using comics and graphic novels in the classroom.          **Stephen Cary**

## Graphic Novels and Curriculum Integration
http://members.shaw.ca/yaying/518final/integ.html
> "Introducing graphic novels that address history, politics, literature, or social issues in a comic style format into the school library or classroom may begin to help to bridge the gap between what students want and what schools require"          **ESL Teaching in Canada**

## Information for Teachers and Teacher-Librarians
www.informationgoddess.ca/Comics&GraphicNovels/teachers&tls.htm
> Are you interested in resources for teaching your students:
> - more about visual literacy?
> - how to interpret the finer point of visual texts?
> - how to produce their own comics?          **(Canadian website)**

## Comic Books for Young Adults - A Guide for Librarians
http://ublib.buffalo.edu/lml/comics/pages/
> 'As educators become increasingly aware of the importance of different learning styles, it is clear that comic books can be a powerful tool for reaching visual learners.'          **Michael R Lavin**

## Graphic Novels - a visual literary art form
www.clermont.lib.oh.us/graphic_novels.html
> What is most exciting is that a picture language and a word language can interweave, which can't be done by either one alone."          **Will Eisner, Clermont County Public Library**

## Shakespeare Learning Commons
www.canadianshakespeares.ca/learningcommons.cfm
> The Shakespeare Learning Commons is a new resource on the CASP website that aims to be the largest collection of teaching and learning resources related to Shakespeare on the Internet. This release is a small taste of what is to come as we continue to develop resources that use adaptation theory to study and teach about Shakespeare's work and their cultural effects.          **Canadian Adaptations of Shakespeare Project**

## The Secret Origin of Good Readers
www.night-flight.com/secretorigin/index.html
> Discusses how teachers, librarians, retailers, and publishers can work together to bring comic books into the classroom for use as an innovative and motivating cross-curricular teaching tool and a vehicle for promoting reading and literacy.

# MAKING COMICS AND GRAPHIC NOVELS:-
**National Association of Comic Art Educators**

www.teachingcomics.org/curriculum.php

> One of the primary the goals of NACAE is to assist educational institutions and individual educators interested in establishing a comics art curriculum. Excellent links, and papers on the topic of Comics in the Classroom.                    **NACAE**

**Scrap Comics**

http://escrapbooking.com/projects/scrapcomic/index.htm

> 'Let's use picture books, sequential art, and comics as tools for teaching critical thinking skills related to sequencing across the curriculum.'                    **Eduscapes**

# GENERAL GRAPHIC NOVEL SITES:-
**Graphic Novel Review Site for Teens**

www.noflyingnotights.com

> 'From my subjective point of view, comics represent something between traditional art screenplays, and films - they're visual like art and film, but they are full of dialogue and short description like screenplays.' Covers everything from superheroes to historical novels via Manga and cartoons.                    **Robin Brenner**

**Parchment of Light: The Life & Death of William Shakespeare**

www.canadianshakespeares.ca/multimedia/imagegallery/craine.cfm

> 'Craine's method of depicting and adapting the life of William Shakespeare reveals a powerful and comprehensive approach to the life of the Bard, encompassing the theatre as medium (brought to life in graphic novel form), facts, conjecture, allegory, interpretation and song lyrics by The Clash.'                    **Nick Craine**

# SHAKESPEARE IN ACTION:-
**Join the debate**

www.shakespeareday.com

> What greater role model for the people of Great Britain? Should we not have a day to recognise this home grown genius?

**British Shakespeare Company**

www.britishshakespearecompany.com/history.html

> The tradition of open-air theatre is deeply rooted in British culture. As the leading exponent in this field The British Shakespeare Company have established major Shakespeare festivals for Brighton, Nottingham, Leeds, The Royal Botanic Gardens at Kew, Cannizaro Park in Wimbledon and in the West End at the world-famous Holland Park Theatre. The team are also filming scenes from The Tempest, a major project for all involved. The British Shakespeare Company, now in its 12th year, has achieved critical acclaim for its productions throughout the country, and is Europe's leading exponent of open-air theatre.

**London Shakespeare Workout**

www.londonshakespeare.org.uk/lsw/

> By virtue of an ever burgeoning series of varied incentives, actors, film-makers alongside offenders and ex-offenders of all ages, genders, races, creeds, nationalities and orientations are given opportunities to further explore and develop skills of self-expression and jointly enhance confidence through the glorious balm which is Shakespeare's language, as well as that of other major dramatic voices and thinkers and film-makers who have been inspired by the Bard throughout time.

**Shakespeare 4 Kidz**

www.shakespeare4kidz.com/

> For over 10 years S4K have been providing a unique insight to the world of William Shakespeare for children all over the UK and across the globe! Their acclaimed approach has proved a hit with kidz and adults alike.

**Public Theater - Shakespeare in the Park**

www.publictheater.org/view.php?mode=eventdisplay&eventid=210

> Performances taking place in Central Park, New York

**Bristol Shakespeare Festival**

http://bristolshakespeare.homestead.com/

> Every summer, one of the UK's largest open air Shakespeare festivals takes place in Bristol. In the beautiful parks and green spaces of the city, professional companies from all over the country perform between May and August

**Shakespeare's Globe**

www.frontofmind.co.uk/

> Together, the Globe Theatre Company, Shakespeare's Globe Exhibition and Globe Education seek to further the experience and international understanding of Shakespeare in performance.

# SHAKESPEARE GENERAL INTEREST:-

**Shakespeare Magazine**

http://shakespearemag.com/

> You've come to the right place if you teach Shakespeare, talk about Shakespeare, go to Shakespeare productions and films, or just plain love Shakespeare. A Magazine for Teachers and enthusiasts alike.

**Shaksper - the Global Electronic Shakespeare Conference**

www.shaksper.net/

> The international electronic conference for Shakespearean researchers, instructors, students, and those who share their academic interests and concerns.

**Shakespeare Birthplace Trust**

www.shakespeare.org.uk/

> The Shakespeare Birthplace Trust is considered the most significant Shakespeare charity in the world. Formed in 1847 with the purchase of Shakespeare's Birthplace, the Trust has since acquired four other houses relating to Shakespeare, for which they care, for the benefit of the nation.

## Mr William Shakespeare and the Internet

http://shakespeare.palomar.edu/

> 'Aims to be an annotated guide to the scholarly Shakespeare resources available on the Internet. Admittedly, some of the resources are not so scholarly, but that's as may be. Usefulness to students (in the broadest sense) is most often the guiding principle. The truly un-scholarly sites are linked on the "Other" Sites page. One very popular feature is a listing of Shakespeare Festivals.'

## Internet Shakespeare Editions

http://internetshakespeare.uvic.ca/index.html

> 'The aim of the Internet Shakespeare Editions is to inspire a love of Shakespeare's works in a world-wide audience. To do so, we create and publish works for the student, scholar, actor, and general reader in a form native to the medium of the Internet.'

## Shakespeare Resource Center

www.bardweb.net/

> You'll find here collected links from all over the World Wide Web to help you find information on William Shakespeare. There are millions of pages that reference Shakespeare on the Internet. This American site aims to make it a little easier to find your sources.

## The Shakespeare Society of Southern Africa

www.ru.ac.za/institutes/isea/shake/

> The Shakespeare Society strives to serve the interests of a wide variety of sectors, from school pupils, students and teachers, to ordinary Shakespeare enthusiasts, academics, theatrical people and cultural workers.

## The Shakespeare Mystery

www.pbs.org/wgbh/pages/frontline/shakespeare/

> Who in fact was Shakespeare? The debate continues.

## Interactive Folio and Study Guide for Romeo and Juliet

www.canadianshakespeares.ca/rjfolio.cfm

> Here you'll find quite simply the most interactive and sophisticated version of Romeo and Juliet ever created. Use this as a study guide and teaching tool. Read the play, read its English source texts, read critical materials on the play, explore Shakespeare's vocabulary, and experience a full range of multi-media associated with the play.  **Canadian Adaptations of Shakespeare Project**

# SHAKESPEARE ASSOCIATIONS:-

## The British Shakespeare Association

www.britishshakespeare.ws/

> The BSA was formed in 2003 and is dedicated to supporting people who teach, research and perform Shakespeare's works.

## The Shakespeare Society of Japan

www.s-sj.org/english/index.html

> The Shakespeare Society of Japan annually publishes a refereed journal, Shakespeare Studies, in English.